TANGO

Poetry of Buenos Aires

FILING BIBLIOGRAPHY

Title: Tango, poetry of Buenos Aires

Author: Horacio Salas

Prologue: Horacio Salas

Texts: Roberto Arlt, Leónidas Barletta, León Benarós y otros.

Content: Thoughts and feelings in connection with tango, related by writters and poets.

Characteristics: 152 pages, 23 x 31 cm

Editor: © 1998 Manrique Zago ediciones S.R.L., Buenos Aires

TANGO
POETRY OF BUENOS AIRES

© 1998 Manrique Zago ediciones S.R.L.
Pte. Luis Sáenz Peña 232 - (1110) Buenos Aires - República Argentina
Tel 382-8880, 383-9038 / 39 - Telefax: (54-1) 383-9055

E-mail: mzago@lvd.com.ar
www.mzago.com.ar

ISBN 987-509-038-7

TANGO
POETRY OF BUENOS AIRES

Manrique Zago
Publishing Direction

Texts
Roberto Arlt, Leónidas Barletta, León Benarós, Eladia Blázquez, Adolfo Bioy Casares, Jorge Luis Borges, Enrique Cadícamo, Miguel A. Camino, Cátulo Castillo, Julio Cortázar, Humberto Costantini, Carlos de la Púa, Marcelino Del Mazo, Enrique Santos Discépolo, Samuel Eichelbaum, Florencio Escardó, Miguel D. Etchebarne, Horacio Ferrer, Celedonio Flores, Waldo Frank, Carlos Fuentes, Manuel Gálvez, Francisco García Jiménez, Alberto Girri, José Gobello, Joaquín Gómez Bas, Raúl González Tuñón, Ricardo Güiraldes, Conde Hermann von Keyserling, Carlos Ibarguren, Leopoldo Lugones, Homero Manzi, Leopoldo Marechal, Ezequiel Martínez Estrada, Victoria Ocampo, Nicolás Olivari, Pedro Orgambide, Hipólito Jesús Paz, Ulyses Petit de Murat, José Portogalo, Fernando Quiñones, Ernesto Sabato, Horacio Salas, Máximo Sanz, Fernán Silva Valdés, José Sebastián Tallon, Alberto Vacarezza, Carlos Vega, Bernardo Verbitsky, Héctor Yánover.

Plastic Works
Carlos Alonso, Martiniano Arce, Jorge Luis Borges, Bourse Herrera, Carlos Cañás, Ricardo Carpani, Juan Carlos Castagnino, Natalia Cohen, Miguel A. D'Arienzo, Gabriel Di Toto, Zdravko Ducmelic, Faruk, Horacio Ferrer, Oscar Giuliani, Fernando Guibert, Jorge Iglesias, Carlos Páez Vilaró, Lino Palacio, Sigfredo Pastor, Máximo Paz, Alfredo Plank, Leopoldo Presas, Hermenegildo Sábat, Vicente Salatino, Aldo Severi, Graciela Shalev, Raúl Soldi, Carlos Torrallardona, León Untroib.

Photographers
Jack Tucmanián, Jorge Luis Campos, Horacio Forlano, Graciela Gracía Romero, Elizabeth Goujon, Eduardo Longoni, S. Rimathé, Pedro Roth, Jorge Salatino.

English Updating
Martín Gallardo

Editorial Production
Mariana Vicat

Design by
Estudio de Diseño Gráfico Valle-Mercado

Industrial Production
Pablo Salvá

Manrique Zago

Pages 4-5: The Central Station, circa 1890.

Shusheta

*And in the afternoons in Palermo
he went for a ride,
and looking for a dream
the porteño conquistador
went past...*

Lyrics by Enrique Cadícamo
Music by Juan Carlos Cobián

Fog of the Riachuelo

*Shady anchorage
where ships are put in
and will stay there for ever,
shadows which are lengthening
in the night of pain
shipwrecked people of the world
who have lost their heart...*

Lyrics by Enrique Cadícamo
Music by Juan Carlos Cobián

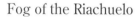

Ships in the mouth of the Riachuelo.

6

My Corrientes...Tough street,
heart of Buenos Aires!
I feel terribly snubbed
and your change shocked me.

Lyrics by Francisco García Jiménez
Music by Aníbal Troilo

Corner of Reconquista and Corrientes. 1910.

Mural painting by Carlos Terribili, based upon texts of
Alejandro Dolina. Flores Station.

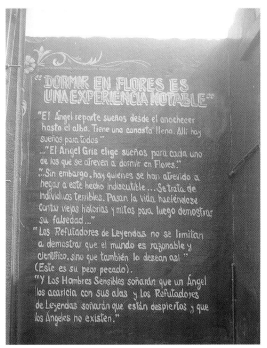

11

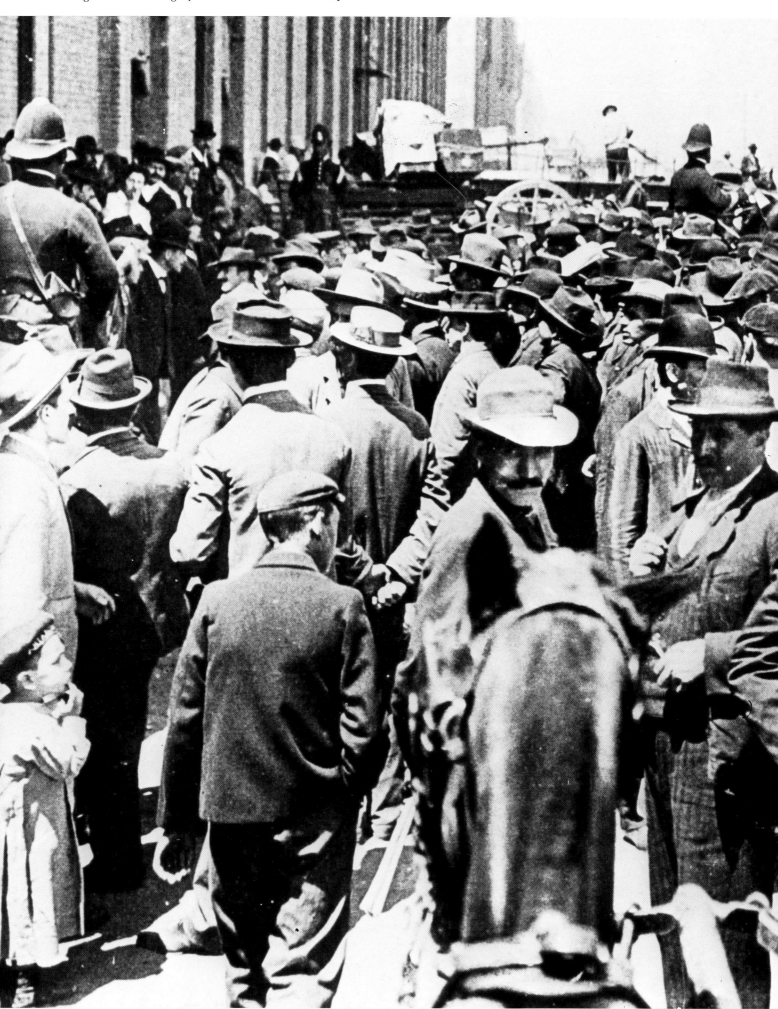

Pages before:
Panoramic view of Avenida 9 de Julio.

Florida Street, by S. Rimathé. 1890.

Aerial view of Florida Street, 1998

Prologue

A sad thought that is danced

Leopoldo Marechal holds that tango *"is an endless possibility"*; Jorge Luis Borges relates it with the "heroic deed of the knife and courage"; Ernesto Sabato believes it is *"the most original phenomenon of the Río de la Plata"* and Enrique Santos Discépolo, one of its greatest creators, defines it as a *"sad thought that is danced"*. The fact is that this is a music that, throughout a century, has become synonym of the country which gave it birth, and has been identified as a typical Argentine characteristic.

As every myth, tango shows a dark, uncertain origin, and as there is a lack of documentation and witnesses, there is no other choice but to appeal to imagination and conjectures.

Let us think of a bonfire in a square full of carts or any public dance on the outskirts. The character, a musician with a good ear who entertains his audience with the sound of a violin, an old clarinet, or a worn guitar. Somebody asks for a little tango and whistles the opening bars which were heard in a public dance of black people and while he was there, he tries some contortions by way of a joke. For the musician, the rhythm sounds like a habanera with which he is so familiar, and the result shows a touch of this music coming from the Caribbean. Another well-meaning listener intervenes and corrects. His humming sounds more like a milonga. Later, somebody with a good memory plays again the hybrid music and the version starts changing. It is like a game in which the players do not realize they have given birth to a myth.

From this conjectural birth, circa mid-1870s, tango moved first to the "cuartos de *chinas*", near the military quarters, where, on Sundays, it was danced from early evening. Later, it moved to the suburban brothels which had spread out on the outskirts owing to the fact that most of immigration was made up of men on their own and many of them were unable to communicate because of the language.

Apart from being the brothels' favorite dance, up to the turn of the century, tango was commonly danced by male couples, to the rhythm of little street organs playing a few melodies. The scene, which was common on the outskirts, was described by Evaristo Carriego

in a famous poem: *On the street the good people squander/ their rude, flattering words/ because to the beat of tango which is* La Morocha *they stand out in agile steps of borderline men.*

At first, it was played by trios of flute, violin and guitar which were easily portable instruments in harmony with the musicians' trekking through different bars. But soon tango counted with the participation of a new instrument: the bandoneon, a sort of concertina which was created with the intention of replacing the organ during the religious rural services by Heinrich Band, in Hamburg, in 1835. In a short time, the bandoneon replaced the flute and became an essential instrument in the interpretation of tango. Says Luis Adolfo Sierra: *"With the gradual elimination of the naughty and picaresque frills of the flute, tango started to lose its original lively and playful character. It then adopted a harsh, rhythmic, austere and subdued temperament. And the bandoneon was, no doubt, the reason for this dramatic change of mood which perhaps what the tango waited for to become a plaintive and sentimental music."* Later, and only in a few dance halls or brothels, some pianos were shyly added.

The milieu where this phenomenon took place, already deep-rooted on the outskirts, was populated mainly by settlers from the province who were driven by the economic changes to get closer to the Capital city: odd-job men, dockers, bricklayers, peddlers, greengrocers, slaughtermen, soldiers, show-offs, rogues and, above all, amazed immigrants in search of new horizons.

It was the world of the isolated neighborhoods, areas where borderline *criollos* intermingled with foreigners. Especially people from southern Italy who still dreamed of going back to their homeland after making a fortune in America and, since they could not integrate through language, tried to do it through the notes of tango. This phenomenon spread so much that the Italian names soon prevailed among the first groups of musicians who used to perform in the suburban cafés, in the Vuelta de Rocha. The "Guardia Vieja" was made up of those same men who unwittingly stamped tango with a sad and nostalgic tone, always prevailing in the immigrant's life. On the other hand, when the children of the porteño aristocracy discovered tango in the brothels, they decided to appropriate it. Displaying their macho attitude, they used to fight over prostitutes in the popular dance halls and finally learned the steps of the dance as a childish prank, perhaps even a temporary fashion. It was them who took the figures of tango to Europe. They made it wear tails and showed it in Paris. And there, without the damaging effect of its origins, or perhaps because of this very sinful feel, tango became an allowed transgression and was a complete success.

These wealthy Argentineans, who were the owners of the meat, wheat and pampas where the gaucho was born, with a Latin-lover fame, who were able to squander a considerable fortune in a few months on a spree, finally imposed their exotic music. In Europe, dozens of dance academies emerged in order to teach this new dance and the word tango was all the rage. There were "tango teas", "tango color", tango exhibitions. Worried about his officers' morality, Kaiser Wilhelm II of Germany prohibited them to dance it in uniform. In Rome, even Pope Pius X after seeing some of its steps and figures had to give his opinion about the dance that was finally absolved from the sinful character its detractors attributed to it.

On its return from Europe, once tango had become a product that "decent people" could consume, a new environment had to be created in order to enjoy it without going to the underground brothels, rubbing shoulders or fighting with the populace. The rich young men got tired of fighting with the shore line audience and the women who lived of other's money began to proliferate as an inevitable ornament for high society, and as a way of pointing out some life guidelines. Times were changing and, especially from the approval of the 1912 law regarding universal, secret and obligatory vote, a social mix was presaged which made it necessary to establish a number of rules of behavior in order to avoid confusions. That is how the first exclusive cabarets were born, such as the famous Armenonville.

The prediction announcing a change in the Argentine political scene turned out to be correct. In 1916, with the first presidential elections which took place within the democratic framework of the Sáenz Peña Law, power changed hands. Hipólito Yrigoyen, the undisputed leader of the Unión Cívica Radical party, was elected president of the Argentine Republic and with him, the middle class began to participate for the first time in the Argentine political life.

A break was made in the former domains of oligarchy. The inhabitants of the humble neighborhoods, the immigration's sons and grandsons, together with old *criollos* who were not involved with the patrician circles, were struggling to make progress from the beginning of the century, and started to participate in this new period.

On the other hand, a significant change in the development of tango was made almost simultaneously. Until then, it had been a music only meant to support the dance; the few known lyrics were only brothel verses which could not be sung in any other place or some naive, rural verses such as those of *La morocha*, by Angel Villoldo and music by Saborido. But only five months before the beginning of the Yrigoyen Administration, the tango-song was created, and the history of this music changed.

In February 1917, Carlos Gardel, a singer born in Toulouse, France, and who arrived in Buenos Aires at the age of three, dared to sing in front of an audience for the first time, on the stage of the Esmeralda Theatre, the lyrics of a tango. He sang the verses which were added by Pascual Contursi to the old theme by Samuel Castriota, *Lita*, that was renamed *Mi noche triste*. To top it all, these lyrics were splashed with *lunfardo* in which a pimp moaned about his protégée's abandoning. However, the combination of the lyrics and Gardel's wonderful and personal voice started the change. Soon, thousands of records were sold and from that moment, Gardel left aside the country songs that were his specialty to become the archetype of a new porteño character: the tango singer.

The success of this new kind of music, the transformation from a pure dance to a song, reached the theaters and every Spanish farce in Buenos Aires included at least one new tango with lyrics. The actors became singers and the records and scores were published with a great success. New small orchestras of huge popularity emerged, such as Julio De Caro's and Osvaldo Fresedo's, and despite its origins, tango was accepted in family homes.

It was the time when the *porteño* inhabitants slowly began to discover their own city. The intelligentsia, mesmerized so far by Paris, began to look at the daily landscape; they saw that this context could be the subject of their works and the city was introduced in the pages of their books. It began to take shape. Baldomero Fernández Moreno adopted it as the protagonist of his works; his way of describing it was simple and conveyed the minimal events which were discovered during his long walks in the neighborhoods; Jorge Luis Borges, who had just arrived from a long journey through Europe, showed his city passion even in the title of his first book: *Fervor de Buenos Aires,* and inquired into the suburban characters, i.e. the *guapos* and *compadres* who became the characters of many of his future stories. Likewise, other poets such as Raúl González Tuñón, Nicolás Olivari, Oliverio Girondo and Leopoldo Marechal observed the *porteño* streets and tango filtered into several of their works.

Reviled, at first, due to their tiresome insistence on the subject of the abandonment (which was caused by the initial success of *Mi noche triste* and the lack of imagination of Contursi's followers), or criticized in an ironic way because of its schmaltzy tones, tango lyrics were sung by different sectors of the population. Their stories became part of Buenos Aires' daily routine. They reflected a world which was still amazed by the end of the *belle époque* and the impact caused by World War I. A world that still dragged on —and would drag on for many years— the prejudices imposed as a rule by the Victorian empire in the second half of the 19th century.

Most of the lyricists of the beginning of the tango-song were simple versifiers with an abi-

lity for improvisation, a good sense of rhymes, or playwrights who were forced to include tangos in their plays. But when you see them from a distance you can tell that they were able to reflect their environment and their time. And despite their academic limitations, they did it fine. In such a way that —as Borges said— the whole process discovers an epic. A *summa* that gathers a wide range of characters and feelings, from the *compadrito* to the cabaret habitué; from the suburban rogue to the rich kid; from the suburban photography and the neighborhood pride to the guilt feeling, the anxiety about the uncertain future or the fear of loneliness.

At the end of the first period, two poets arrived: Celedonio Flores, who showed the contrast between high society's life and the meek's morality; Enrique Cadícamo, who was concerned about life in cabarets, the historical chronicle and the description of sentimental moments; Homero Manzi, whose mark was the neighborhood nostalgia and lost characters, as well as the depth of love affairs; Cátulo Castillo, who was the poet of evocations, the alcohol drama and elegy; Homero Espósito, who described the porteño's social and psychological changes as from the 1940s, and Enrique Santos Discépolo who gave tango a hopeless, skeptical vision and made it a thoughtful and metaphysical music, establishing a number of ethical standards that reflected a wide range of feelings, all the way from personal pains deep in his heart to the reality of a sociopolitical situation ruled by a lack of morality.

More recently, the verses by Eladia Blázquez which are more suitable for the new city reality, its inhabitants and problems, and by Horacio Ferrer, who shows an accurate use of surprising metaphors, deeply rooted, however, in the best tango and city tradition, emerged from the poetic scene of tango.

An image of reality

On September 6, 1930, the porteños woke up with the sound of precarious airplanes which dropped some pamphlets announcing the revolution that took place a few hours later. At sunset, General José Félix Uriburu leading the cadets from the Military School, entered the *Casa Rosada*, seized power in a coup, dissolved Parliament and inaugurated a long series of military coups which characterized during more than fifty years the Argentine political life.

At the same time, an obscure, repetitive era began for Tango, just as it happened for the country, splashed with a number of achievements by Discépolo which were only known by the end of the 1930s with the appearance of new orchestras and the large-scale spreading of new tangos (which are currently seen as classics) that were the answer to a new vision of the *porteño* music in agreement with the next social changes. It is the period marked by the names of Aníbal Troilo, Osvaldo Pugliese, Miguel Caló, Horacio Salgán and Homero Manzi's best poems *(Barrio de tango, Sur, Che bandoneón, Malena, Fuimos)*.

The migration of people from the countryside to the city, which had begun a few years before, increased when the government was entrusted to the Peronism. The promising working conditions in the industrial area acted as a hypnotic agent for these waves of men and women coming from the interior who would settle on the outskirts of Buenos Aires. These new sociopolitical protagonists also brought their own music and tango hegemony had to make room to the energy of the melodies coming from the provinces.

New rhythms, dances which seemed foreign to the porteño, seized the city. Meanwhile, tango seemed to fade away. But the resurgence of the music of Buenos Aires could already be seen in the revolutionary and transgressing compositions by a musician with a sound academic training, Astor Piazzolla. He sparked off fierce controversy, and his music had come in for a great deal of criticism and was only admired by a small group of people. It was a tough situation, but at the end of the 1960s, his efforts produced results and the rebirth of tango was already a fact thanks to Roberto Goyeneche's voice —today a popular myth— and the emergence of an excellent singer: Susana Rinaldi.

Another milestone in tango history was reached in 1990 with the foundation of the Academia Nacional del Tango through a Presidential decree, with a similar purpose to that of, for example, the Academy of Arts, Right, Beau-Arts, Science, Education. It was the official act in recognition of the importance of tango to the Argentine culture.

Such a phenomenon, which emerged more than a century ago, could not be avoided by the great writers who are —as it is well-known— those who read best the reality of people. And tango, even in an incidental way, as an accompaniment, appeared in and still emerges from many pages of those authors who tried to investigate the country or discover the most profound sense of the events that have marked the Argentine life. The purpose of this book, which is an homage paid by the Culture Secretariat of Buenos Aires' City Government to Carlos Gardel, is to show a large panorama of opinions about tango and its relationship with the city and its characters. In order to achieve this objective, not only the participation of first-rate Argentine writers such as Borges, Sabato, Cortázar, Marechal, Victoria Ocampo or Adolfo Bioy Casares, among many others, has been included but also that of foreign authors who have occasionally written about tango, its protagonists or climates, such as Waldo Frank, Count Keysserling, Carlos Fuentes or the Spanish writer Fernando Quiñones who, shocked by the death of Esthercita Dalto who inspired the tango *Milonguita*, wrote a poem of which the most significant excerpt has been reproduced here.

This work not only helps to understand tango but also the city which gave it birth, sheltered it and contributed to its development.

Horacio Salas

One

*Full of hopes one looks for
the way his yearnings
have been promised to his dreams...
He knows it is a cruel and long
fight, but he fights and bleeds
determined by his faith...*

Lyrics by E. Santos Discépolo
Music by Mariano Mores

Carnaval porteño, *by the Grupo Muralista del
Oeste, on Independencia Avenue and Bolívar St.*

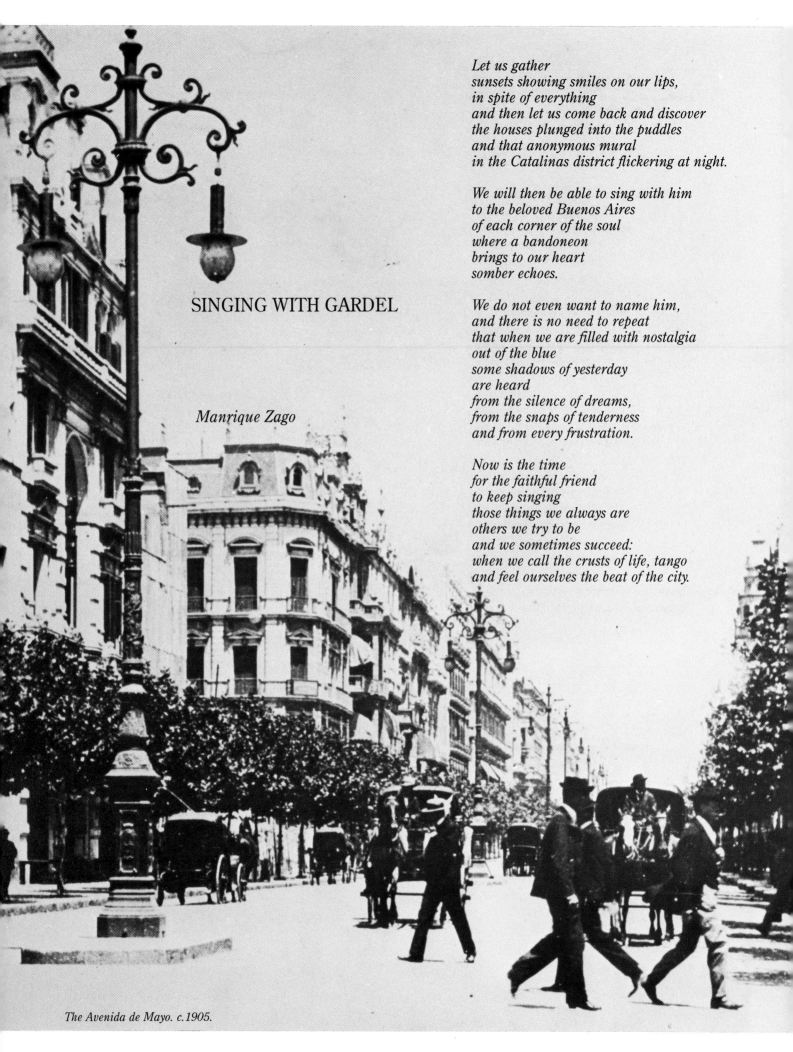

SINGING WITH GARDEL

Manrique Zago

Let us gather
sunsets showing smiles on our lips,
in spite of everything
and then let us come back and discover
the houses plunged into the puddles
and that anonymous mural
in the Catalinas district flickering at night.

We will then be able to sing with him
to the beloved Buenos Aires
of each corner of the soul
where a bandoneon
brings to our heart
somber echoes.

We do not even want to name him,
and there is no need to repeat
that when we are filled with nostalgia
out of the blue
some shadows of yesterday
are heard
from the silence of dreams,
from the snaps of tenderness
and from every frustration.

Now is the time
for the faithful friend
to keep singing
those things we always are
others we try to be
and we sometimes succeed:
when we call the crusts of life, tango
and feel ourselves the beat of the city.

The Avenida de Mayo. c.1905.

My beloved Buenos Aires

Myths and legends

Leopoldo Marechal

The tango carousel

That same night just as dawn was breaking, Megafón had the experience or dream he told me later and that I will call now, The Tango Carousel. Before including this saga of the "Obscure One" in my story, I hesitated a lot as I questioned whether these events were real. But the memories of Macedonio Fernández prevailed, when the porteño metaphysician, in some deserted corner of Adrogué, documented the harmonious continuity of man through his different states and crossed, lying on his bed, the borders of his wakefulness with his dreams and those of his dreams with his wakefulness. These thoughts urged me to capture the vision of the "Obscure One" and transcribe it in this second rhapsody.

It took place, if visions really have a time and place, when Megafón, having abandoned me to my evocative lust, was slowly coming back from Saavedra to his little house in the neighborhood of Flores through the deserted streets of the neighborhood and at the time when night becomes darker with the intention of being the rise of a new day. According to Villa Crespo's "Autodidact", it was on arriving at the intersection of San Pedrito street and Tandil street, when that ghostly music that seemed to emerge from the corner itself, came to his attention. He soon recognized the tango, *Nueve de Julio* —transcribed into terrible dodecaphonic scales— old and tearful with a fossil sentimentalism, and as stuttered by broken bandoneons loosing air through their devastated gums. However, if one bears in mind that there was just a vacant lot on that corner, Megafón headed for that impossible source of music. On entering the vacant lot, he discovered two facts: the place seemed to be filled with a kind of very faint phosphoric light and the tango resounded louder there. Suddenly, the light gained in intensity, and the "Autodidact" saw in its very center a suburban, horse-drawn carousel revolving slowly around to the beat of the tango; the old blindfolded chesnut made the huge thing turn round with its sad, sore back. Some unidentified riders of the wooden horses and swans were also turning around under the inquisitive look of two characters who were standing next to the carou-

Bailando el tango *by*
Fernando Guibert, ink

sel and who were, as Megafón knew later, a demon called Ben and a demon called Nelson. The old chesnut began to slow down, and the carousel as well, as the music came to an end. As soon as silence and immobility were absolute, the demon called Ben spoke to the riders on whose thighs one could see a bandoneon.

—Gentlemen—, he said triumphantly, —it's useless to keep spinning this carousel. Tango is dead! It's not necessary to make an encephalogram or issue a death certificate for its widow: the corpse, traditionally shrouded in percale, sleeps or rots now in the West Cemetery, next to the grave of Carlitos, the immortal, and will not be brought back to life so easily. Listen, you miserable *malevos*! The rhythm of Buenos Aires is no longer in the two-four beat.

As he heard him, the demon named Nelson went pale in his own phosphorescence:

—He lies! —he exclaimed. —The one who has just spoken is a music cheat! Tango is not dead, because, as the great Contursi used to say, everything is lost and nothing is transformed.

At that point the bandoneonists on horseback began to talk loudly, and the old chesnut colored horse turned his ears towards them:

—In my opinion, and if we are at a round table, —explained the Weedy Bandoneonist, —tango is not dead: it's only in a damn coma. Maestros, there's no reason to whine; let's look for those who are responsible! I accuse.

—Whom do you accuse, skinny?,— asked the demon named Ben.

—The mechanic civilization!—, roared the Weedy Bandoneonist. —Habanera, candombe or milonga, tango has always had a rhythm of popular blood in its roots. And who has wasted it? The machine and its piston racket!

The old chesnut colored horse fervently intervened.

—The mechanic drive, —he said, —is a great conquest of civilization. Although it has not reached me, I am a technocracy fan and a sepoy of Imperialism.

—Would you shut up, old nag?—, replied the demon called Ben. —Perhaps you would like to end up in a canning plant?

At that point, the demon called Nelson burst into tears.

—¿What's going on?—, asked the demon called Ben, somewhat surprised.

—I am crying in front of Carlitos Gardel's grave, —whined the demon called Nelson. —The mechanic civilization! If instead of traveling by plane he would have travelled on foot or by car, our thrush would still be alive!

But the Fat Bandoneonist, who was riding a pink swan, looked resentfully at the Sanguine Bandoneonist who was boastfully riding his violet swan.

—What has cocked tango up, —he grumbled, —is those harmony and counterpoint classes. Tango died technically in classroom B of the National Conservatory of Music.

—Yes!, —applauded the demon called Nelson. —In my opinion, the bandoneonist who has just spoken has struck the right note.

—Are you saying this because of me?,— asked the Sanguine Bandoneonist, defiantly.

—Tango is not Nicholas Paganini!,— agreed the Fat Bandoneonist.

—It isn't Rigoletto either!

When he said these words, the belligerent eyes of the Sanguine Bandoneonist lit up with a stroke of genius:

—If we are in the Final Judgment,— he threatened, —even the dead will hear me! ¿What could I do with my bandoneon? ¿Keep draining the sentimental snots of an anachronism with sinusitis?

—The one on the pink swan is right,— encouraged the demon called Ben. —The tears extracted from the bandoneons already threat to dehydrate our brave fellow citizens.

—You are insulting Carlitos' memory! protested the demon named Nelson. —The two-four beat will never die: Carlitos himself explained it to me on the corner of Boedo street and Rivadavia.

—And who denies it?,— grumbled the Sanguine Bandoneonist. —If a Buenos Aires of a sentimental marrow has been replaced by an abstract Buenos Aires, I will set Pythagoras' theorem, Einstein's equation, the preamble to the National Constitution and the generals' mustache without humanism to music!

The heroic overexcitement of the Sanguine Bandoneonist moved his audience. And the old chesnut was the first to react:

—Well said!,— he exclaimed. —Hit the generals hard! The military government exports horse meat to the Japanese!

—Silence, skinny old nag! ordered the demon named Ben.

—Aren't we in a democracy?,— protested the horse.

—This animal is delirious—, laughed the demon. —I would ask when did it vote for the last time. Anyway, neither democracy nor horse meat were asked to stick their nose in this luxurious tango funeral. Gentlemen, even I doubt the very survival of the bandoneon!

At that moment, the demon called Nelson seemed to loose control:

—He is blaspheming!—, he shouted. —At the beginning, in the middle and the end of Buenos Aires, there was, is and will be Arola's bandoneon!

—And what could the already classic sob of the Bandoneon be replaced by?,— asked a bandoneonist who was seated on a yellow swan.

—By the laugh of a trumpet!—, shouted the demon called Ben. —Trumpet, trumpetist, trumpeteer! Cha cha!"

And he began to dance next to the carousel.

—Yankees go home!,— roared the Fat Bandoneonist. —They stole the trumpet to the black man, after beating him to a pulp!

—Why don't the masters of the north stop pestering with useless trumpets!— condemned and flattered the traitorous horse. —And may they continue to produce their wonderful HH.PP. !

Then, there was a small pandemonium in the place. The hideous entity named Ben accelerated his trunk contortions and the movement of his dancing legs.

—Trombone, trombonist!,— he wailed. —The leaf-trombone and the fruit-trombone! And, yeah!

—Death to Jazz Imperialism!,— shouted the Weedy Bandoneonist using up all his pneumatic capacity in this effort.

While the infernal entity called Nelson put out his damned hand to the infernal entity called Ben, the Fat Bandoneonist, between two riders who held him, tried to get off his swan and throw himself ready to cause a slaughter.

The Carousel

*The carousel on the
dark corner cries
and the things which once
were roses bleed...*

Lyrics by Cátulo Castillo
Music by Mariano Mores

But, at that moment, the Sanguine Bandoneonist produced with his instrument a hurricane of loud and high-pitched notes which left everybody paralyzed and confused.

—This music,— he said, —belongs to my last tango, and is a *mea culpa* of old mistakes.

—Are you accusing the maestros?,— asked the demon called Ben. —I accuse the tango lyricists!

—And what are you accusing them of?, — asked the demon called Nelson.

—Of putting into circulation a fauna of whining malevos, gutsy and cuckold young men and *milonguitas* who, whether dressed in percale or in grey foxes, dragged in this city a terribly tough *karma*.

—He is destroying the myths of Buenos Aires!,— shouted the demon named Nelson full of rage. —The accuser is a tricky prosecutor, and we need a defense counsel with no strings attached! Let us summon here the great George!

—The Great George won't be able to come,– announced the demon called Ben: —he is mending fogs in Great Britain. But if the jury has any doubt whatsoever, this public prosecutor will call his witnesses.

As if he were wrapped in an invisible gown, the demon called Ben put out his hand to the forum of the vacant lot, where the phosphorescent light seemed as solid as a zinc sheet. And, standing out against it, a man figure suddenly jumped and moved forward as far as the carousel, brandishing a poor conventional dagger. The specter was sporting a grey hat, a jacket and tight-fitting trousers as conventional as the dagger. On seeing him, a number of laudatory voices resounded among those who were riding wooden swans or little horses:

—It's the *Cafiolo Vidalita*!
—The *Ciruja*!
—Puente Alsina!

With his eyes full of tears, the entity called Nelson summoned the ghost and said to him:

—Venerable shadow, for Filiberto's harmonium, I beg you to tell us your name!

—I'm none of the undersigned,— explained the ghost. —I am here as a union delegate. And I would like to know who was the stiff poet who put us in the union.

—Has the witness a statement to make?,— asked the demon called Ben.

—Mister prosecutor,— claimed the ghost, —what right do they have to put me up in some den full of bows and with uncomfortable guitars which could hardly be hung up in a closet?

—That's not true!,—refuted the demon named Nelson. —A Creole guitar, according to physics, can hang up in a closet without transgressing the laws of gravity.

—And what right do they had,— insisted the ghost, —to give us all the trappings of fierceness, only to look in front of the people as a perfect cuckold?

—There certainly were reasons for that,"—said the demon called Ben.

—Which ones? A chick, a woman or a figurine who walked away in a luxurious *voiturette* to the Armenonville.

—The 'lights of downtown'!,— deplored here the demon called Nelson, as an elegy.

—The specter is right!,— said the old chestnut, showing a tender support.

—He will be,— replied the demon called Ben, —when the witness explains to us if what walked away in a *voiturette* was a figurine, a woman or a chick without any specific trait.

—And why should I know?,— grumbled the ghost. –Check with the Royal Academy of *Lunfardo*!

But at that moment, an infuriated old woman jumped from the back of the zinc sheet brandishing a broom: she wore a rubber apron, a frayed cap and a scarf in shreds.

—Get out of here, buddies!,— she yelled sweeping away the specter with her broom— Get out, scoundrels!

The demon called Ben carefully studied her:

—Take it easy, grandma,— he ordered with an expression somewhere between cheerfulness and wickedness, —and state your name, address, and profession to the court.

—I'm called the "Poor Little Old Woman," —grumbled the woman with sparkling, bewitching eyes, —or the "Good Little Mother". I lived in lousy, unventilated tango verses. ¿Which was my profession? That of

supporting a group of bums who slept on their beds or learned to play some bandoneons as wretched as my life. And, of course, they kept asking for *mate* at the top of their lungs, at any time of the day or night! And I kept rushing around, poor old woman!, from the burner to the bed and from the bed to the burner.

—Tell us, old woman,— ordered the demon called Ben, —if it is true that all these buddies swung as pendulums from the Parnaso to the police station.

—It is true!,— she whined. —They thought they were geniuses because they rhymed *"tango"* with *"fango"* (mud) and with *"tamango"* (shoe).

The old woman's monologue-elegy had a deep effect on the riders' emotions. Soon after, the entity called Nelson let out an indignant voice.

—Objection!,— he said, —the most sacred thing we human beings have, has just been defiled here: the name of a mother!

On listening to him, the "Poor Little Old Woman" planted herself in front of him, called him every name under the sun, and vanished into thin air doing a few sweeps with her broom.

But who was that ghostly girl emerging from the zinc sheet, moving forward and shining like a Muse?

Riders and demons saw her golden hair and her blue eyes like thistle flowers at noon; and they soon noticed that the figure changed in the air according to the nature of her possible fates. Either she wore the sweet suburban percale (which brought back Esthercita's immortal legend); or she adorned herself with a *cocotte*'s satin and jewels (which reminded the riders the deplorable story of Zorro Gris).

And through her mutations, the figure only kept her wheat-like hair and her forget-me-not-like eyes, a bygone youth laughing at its glories or weeping for its setbacks.

—State your name,— ordered the prosecutor insensible to the ghost's charms.

—I am the Rubia Mireya,— said the witness, —in the good and bad times, in spring or autumn of love.

The Rubia Mireya! Yes, on hearing her hot honey-like voice, the enraptured bandoneonists fell from their saddles.

—Legal address?,— insisted the demon called Ben.

—I lived in or I have been lodged,— answered Mireya, —at the hallways of Chiclana, which are as discreet as caves. Or in the old patios of San Telmo, among a fire of geraniums and hydrangeas. In the dandies' *garçonnière* or the magnates' palace where I was fed only with Coty perfumes. Or among the troublemakers of Parque Patricios who made me stronger with their barbecues. Or in the musical tenement houses where races fought and got along.

Or in the luxurious private rooms of the Armenonville, or in the cold and white room of a white and cold hospital.

While the riders mounted back on their horses in ecstasy, the demon named Nelson, perspiring highly esteemed soul humidities, came nearer to the Rubia Mireya and kissed her ghostly hand.

—Girl!,— he said, —¿What kind of wind made you gradually lose your petals?

—It was that wind with no fixed rules called Love,— answered Mireya.

—And after that?

—Death. Or a true bandoneon defeated by *Jazz* drums.

At that point, the demon called Ben grumbled his discontent.

—The witness makes excessive use of folklore!,— he protested. —Is it true that, due to too much literature, you were introduced as an Ophelia in a trance, in the manner of William Shakespeare; or as a Marguerite Gauthier, in the manner of Alexandre Dumas Jr., with or without the proverbial roses of tuberculosis on your cheeks?

—And why not?,— pointed out the demon named Nelson. —Tango was reaching then the peak of its damn universality!

But the Rubia Mireya didn't listen to them. Whispering an undecipherable poetic language, she slowly headed for the zinc forum.

—Where are you going young lady?,— asked the demon named Nelson.

Carlos Alonso: Elegía, *mixed technique; lyrics by Alberto Girri, music by Homero Manzi.*
Carlos Torrallardona: Sabor de Buenos Aires, *oil painting; lyrics by Carlos Mastronardi, music by Miguel Caló.*

And she sang softly to herself, before disappearing:

I emerged from the Maldonado
and I go back to the Maldonado.

Mireya's disappearance somehow drove the carousel and its riders to a musical despair or left a romance void, which was soon redeemed by a fourth specter emerging from the forum and moving forward with a pathetic determination. It was the figure of a peasant sporting black loose trousers, a southern poncho and leather, accordion-like boots: although he brandished a riding crop, in the other hand, he held a disconcerting suitcase in the eyes of any expert on the subject. The newcomer planted himself in front of the demon called Ben and addressed these key words:

—Mister commissioner, may I?

He offered his hands to the demon called Nelson right away:

—Arrest me, sergeant,— he shouted to him. —and chain me!

The bandoneonists riders, who have gone from an initial astonishment to a sudden recognition, pronounced here the painful name:

—Alberto Arena!

Yes, it was the same drama's hero: he came from the night, barked at by every dog of fate, cuckold in the north but redeemed in the south, bringing his crime to the east and arranging his punishment west. The four cardinal points of tragedy!

—All things considered,— said the Fat Bandoneonist enthusiastically, —Don Alberto's story is a plain fortunate intervention in the subject matter of tango.

—Even though it is not the first,— said the Weedy Bandoneonist. —"La Morocha" also came from the countryside, and rather earlier.

—With one difference,— approved and disapproved the Sanguine Bandoneonist. If "La Morocha" brings us certain freshness from a romantic Pampa, Don Alberto, presents, shrubs in our faces his double first degree murder.

—That's where I wanted to get— said the demon called Ben.

—The hack journalist who sketched Don Alberto's story not only has breached the

pleasant laws of logic but has also violated the dearest rights of civility.

—Could the witness state which was the thesis of his crime?

—She was unfaithful to me and I killed them both!, —replied Alberto Arena with a rage as retrospective as literary.

—Fair enough,— admitted the demon called Ben. —In this regard, the scales work in quite a regular way and show us a legal figure bordering on classicism. But, what do you keep in your suitcase?

—The evidence of infamy!,— roared the peasant.

And as he opened his luggage, he produced two woman plaits and a bloodstained heart which, badly wrapped in a sheet of newspaper, shouted out his sad entrails nature that was not made for that insolent visibility.

—There you are!,— protested the demon called Ben —The natural thing would have been that don Alberto, after his massacre, had buried both corpses in one piece at the foot of an ombu, a perfect place since the ombu is a giant, and technically melancholic, tree. But what did he do? Showing an exhibitionism which was certainly not suitable for his dignity, he cut the plaits of his wifc and ripped off, surgically speaking, the most noble anatomical piece which a surprised lover can feel proud of. Did these elements constitute hard evidence of infamy? No sir! Taking a snapshot of the adulterous act in situ, if possible with two eyewitness, would have been much more effective. And something else: the punitive cut of a woman's plait has always been carried out among us for teaching purposes, that is to say, with a living woman; and never has a genuine *criollo* pulled out postmortem the plaits of his spouse, no matter how sly she was, in view of the incurable futility of the operation. Ah, gentlemen, this has been the first kick logic has ever received in its mathematic bottom!

When the bandoneonists were faced with that speech by the demon called Ben, they turned pale; demon Nelson hesitated over his principles; and the old chestnut, carefully listening with its well oriented ears, seemed to be perturbed now:

I'm walking around Buenos Aires,
singing a tango for Buenos Aires.
Everybody is fighting hand-to-hand for a buck
but I'm singing a tango for Buenos Aires.
I'm going to pick you up
on this chamferless corner in San Telmo...

Lyrics and music by Virgilio and Homero Espósito

Homenaje a Troilo, *mural painting on*
Independencia Avenue and Balcarce St.

Giuliani: "Gordo, gordo, quedate aquí...", *oil painting.*

—I've never trusted the complex human being!,— declared the old horse sententiously. —He has no sense of responsibility and moderation. And I don't even want to think of the Creole horse, my unfortunate brother, that was forced to cross the Pampas that night, carrying on its back a suitcase without honor!

—The horse is right,— continued the demon called Ben triumphantly. —With plenty of common sense, it brings up Don Alberto's suitcase. Members of the court, what does the peaceful entity of a suitcase suggest to us all? The pleasures of tourism, its clothes and cosmetic festivals; and in the end, the furtive pleasures of smuggling. That's what a suitcase tells us in its functional honesty! And what did Don Alberto do? He defiled his, putting macabre cuttings in it which were crying out for the discretion of a morgue! Is the court outraged? You are absolutely right. And, however, Don Alberto didn't stop there: riding roughshod over distinguished human coexistence rules, he arrived with his red package to the door of a rural police station. Gentlemen, I will ask you something: what right did he have to overwhelm with his horns and his funereal suitcase an honorable rural police inspector, perhaps tired of chasing rustlers and chicken thieves, inevitably loaded with children and a woman as spicy as a red pepper? And on who's authority did he demand chains and fetters to an honorable sergeant whose traditional roots get into the humus of Middle Age no less?

—Good Heavens!— The demon called Ben flashed and roared like a fake Jupiter. And Alberto Arena, after picking up his suitcase, began to disappear and dissolve on the zinc background of the vacant lot. But new ghostly creatures, screaming vicissitudes, emerged; and the bandoneonists thought they recognized Garufa and the Girl of the Circus, and Don Esteban, the Chorra, and the philosopher from Uno and the young girl from Pañuelito as well.

—Enough!,— exorcised the demon called Ben. —Get back to your paradises or hells!

And facing the riders:

—Did you finally understand?,— he shouted to them.

Now, when everything seemed to sink into the anxiety of that final judgment, an entity with a bony face and feverish eyes bursted in, and, speaking to the bandoneonists, said:

—Listen, music souls! If tango is dead, you are mourning it with a good reason. And if it's not dead, why are you crying for it? Ineffable malevos, don't lose heart! Tango is an endless possibility.

—Discepolín!,— cried the riders in unison. But the poet soared into the southern night, amid a double fugue of angelic bandoneons. And the riders, as if redeemed, spurred the old chesnut on.

—Here we go with the waterwheel again,—philosophized the old horse. —See you! If you see Elbiamor, tell her I'm very grateful for her prayers for the night horses.

The chesnut started to walk at a snail's pace that became later an unbelievable trot: once again, the carousel was spinning on its axle. And one could see a circle of riders, wooden horses and swans with long necks parading quicker and quicker to the sound of music. Then, the chesnut galloped as if it was injected with Pegassus' hormones. And in the middle of that turmoil of agitated emotions, the demon called Nelson took the pear-shaped piece of quebracho where the bonus ring was inserted, and, offered and denied it to the rotary riders who extended their anxious hands.

Suddenly, the whole vision vanished into thin air: the neighborhood rooster hoisted its first bugle sounds, feathered and pressing leader at the break of dawn.

Nicolás Olivari

Old grocery store "To the City of Genoa"

Old grocery store "To the City of Genoa"
in Cangallo street and Ombú.
Your memory is accompanied by
the memory of my distant childhood
while a *criollo* cuarteador,
—a malevo and girl chaser—
zigzagged along with the jalopy that went as far as Boedo and Europa
that is to say: the end of the world.
And when General Don Julio Argentino Roca, by car,
inaugurated the greatest sewer
kept in the bowels of Cangallo street.
I remember you in the rounds
of your drunkards' choir,
piling up next to your tin bars
where, on a stone slab, as sad as my childhood,
—dark green-stained with elbows and insults—
you could read these quatrains:

    "As my father for giving credit
    inherited me
    the duty to work
    since the day he died.
    If I were given credit
    for my little bills
    I would also give my friends
    credit for the little drinks..."

(Where are you, François Villon, you drifter and crook,
who devoted your inspiration to an alcoholic instant?)
I remember you, Cangallo and Ombú,
with my memory sponged up from the fever of my many diseases,
because I was always ill,
—the threshold of Cangallo has picked up every fever of mine—
my burning which was that of a lizard curled up under the sun of the
number 905,
a sun better than the centennial's for my rachitic bones...
I remember you, Cangallo and Ombú:
My mother was then so young and beautiful!
—The most beautiful woman in the world—.
She rocked me with "La Morocha".
That song was the first Argentine word I ever heard in
the sweet dialect of her lips:

    "I'm La Morocha,
    the prettiest..."

Cangallo and Ombú!
If you are the whole city of memories,

Electric or horse-drawn streetcars. c.1900.

if it is bursting of nostalgia
as the carnations behind Julio's ear —the malevo who killed the little corporal Ibañez— used to burst; as the shots in Balvanera's atri-
um during the tough nationalist elections,
when the Vázquez' with their elastic loot
and their pocket full of money
put identity cards up for auction in the party's office around the corner,
where I went with a look of electoral horror
on my face,
led by the my uncle's hand,
the owner of the "Old Grocery Store of Genoa",
who, imperturbable and as a government supporter,
sold the peach eau-de-vie to the party's office...
General Mitre's funeral
was a prelude to the first socialist demonstrations,
and the chorus of "La Internacional"
—exotic, cosmopolitan and barbarian
as a grappa gargle—.
Cangallo and Ombú,
I've seen the flagging, carved up shadows passing through
your corner,
with a hole on their chest, and an oily mop of hair...
the malevos, the Italians, good drunkards
of my memories.
Miquelín, as big as a statue,
who went to the harvest and returned rich for two weeks
—hardly enough to pay a round for the whole neighborhood—.
He used to sing until he ran out of money,
he sang the far-off milanese songs of his land
and shouldered memories as if shouldering cereal...
But when asking for credit was useless
he began to call names.
He had the bad wine and cursed Our Lady the Virgin Mary,
using vicious words which were swallowed by my porteño avidity.
Loud-mouth tremolos of singers and the *cinchadas* (tug o'war) of
the basque milkmen next to the store.
Picture cards of Vuelta Abajo cigarettes
and smokes from Brazil.
In this mixture crawled my childhood
and that's why I love Buenos Aires so much!
Buenos Aires, devil's hill, Buenos Aires, homeland of the world,
Buenos Aires wide, long and large,
as that first word in Argentine language I heard from my mother:

> "I'm 'La Morocha',
> the prettiest..."

Buenos Aires, river, iron and asphalt morocha!
Buenos Aires. You still are the prettiest city!

Joaquín Gómez Bas

When the heart holds its beats

In the night, when there is neither wind, moon, nor stars, not even dew, the neighborhood shows a spectral, static, frozen landscape everywhere; a landscape especially made for the passage of goblins and skeletons; a landscape lying face down, irremissibly dead, where a howling shriek is expected to be heard along its streets and to increase at every crossroad, shaking the green sleepy privets, the lethargy of the aromos, willows and cedrons and causing the misted up streetlamps hanging on the corners, to jump up and down. Only when the heart holds its beats, one can perceive the stealthy and slow steps of fear on the bricks of a sidewalk, moving forward, invisible, silencing the late cockcrow, the frogs' croak; eliminating the slight rubbing of the fallen leaves, and muffling the barely audible burst of the bubbles decorating the putrid water of the ditches.

It is in this kind of nights when you expect to hear Don Victor's phonograph with its sudden rattle-like shrillness, don Carmelo's guitar strumming, stirring up the still shadows, a dirty song emerging from the rasping voice of some drunkard, the planks' vibration of the bridge, the sound of a scream, a whistle, a shot; any sign of life, any sign of death; anything that may wake up this panorama of crouched terror, of crime lying in wait and ready to jump; whatever, even if it lacks, in its essence, of the plaintive sweetness, the mawkish vibration emerging from that bandoneon which is gasping now in the patio and clearing with its appropriate chords the suspended terror of the neighborhood.

The tango slowly and submissively crawls, following the rhythmic stimulus of the inflamed guitar player who slaps the strings; the absorbed violinist saws the melody, and the third one offers the real stature of the common people's soul, stretching his bandoneon to the full.

The couples contort themselves from the waist down, improving the complicated art of achieving elegance and nimbleness without the essential, solemn gracefulness being affected in any way. In the emergency, Claudio imposes the elegance of his fine strapping appearance and the agile movement of his legs, drawing on the tiled floor the whining arabesque of the little music. Thanks to his patient teaching, I also manage to perform as a nimble dancer, despite the fact that the entertainment is not attractive enough to get really excited about it. My friend explains to me its advantages:

"Dance is stupid when it is performed between men. Of course, you can perform cortes and firuletes, and the girl envies you and respects you... But in a real party, not one single chick will even look at you if you are a poor dancer... Look: I know what I'm talking about... The best way of capturing a girl's heart is to squeeze her tight and never stop dancing... With the dancing trick, everything works... and in the long run, the meat is left on the hook... Ah!, by the way... Yesterday night I took Rosita to my room... Well... What a body, brother! A young filly, even whiter than milk... Jesus!... She left me as a squeezed orange... Are you leaving already? So early? Stay, later we're gambling..."

There are still streetcars in Buenos Aires. 1998.

Sometimes tango gives me back things
of a most cherished time, lost in time,
the rainy afternoons listening to the radio
while the old tree danced in the street.
The streetcar went past, spreading noises...

Lyrics by Oscar del Priore
Music by Armando Pontier

Carlos Fuentes

Shedding skin

One afternoon, Javier and you arranged to meet at the bar in Santa Fe Avenue. It was in January. You remember it because you could hardly walk down the streets. Tar had melted and in some places, a number of planks had been placed from one side of the street to the other for the people to cross it. You had walked the whole afternoon. You had lunch alone. Then you went to Harrod's in order to see some wool fabric to make yourself an autumn tailleur, but on going into the shop through the revolving doors, you kept going round and round, pushing the glass doors until you came back to the street. It was a small rebellion. You felt on your face that humid heat, mixed with the smells you would always associate with B.A., the gas of the Argentine cars, different from any other gas in the world and which is the safest smell in the city, even safer than that of the shops and restaurants, a smell of linen and wool and leather, smell of reheated pizza, barbecues, fried sausage, chitterlings, the slight smell of chocolate ice creams and, above all, or inside everything, the smell coming from the port docks: tar, coal, steam, frozen meat, fertilizers, cattle, wool bales. Why should you think of the woolen tailleur as from January, in the middle of this heat? You walked. They were making a building at the corner of Maipú street and Sarmiento and the workers had stopped to eat something. Some of them were standing on the sidewalk, at the entrance to the building site; others were sitting high up, among the skeleton pillars, as in niches. They were eating a cheese and ham baguette, and some meat. They were drinking wine. They spoke a kind of Spanish with Italian and Polish inflections. You stopped in front of the shop windows. You saw crocodile purses, merino and alpaca fabrics, and *ponchos*. You went into a perfume store in Maipú street. You were offered, in a row, ten or twelve perfumes. You laughed; you used them all. You went out perfumed. You avoided Florida street, closed at that time to traffic. You would loose an hour at the El Ateneo bookstore and would finally get out with a copy of *Martín Fierro* with a leather binding. You took Lavalle street with the intention of seeing the theaters' publicity boards and finding out if there was any new or old film you had not seen yet. They

Muñequitas porteñas, *first Argentine talkie.*

Four different expressions of tango in posters.

were showing, by surprise, old Argentine films which you enjoyed a lot. Awful melodramas, with a lot of tangos, a great deal of nostalgia for the centennial's *Belle Epoque,* a great deal of folklore from the port neighborhoods. You stopped in front of each of the thirty theaters in Lavalle street; you wore a silk orange patterned dress and high-heeled white shoes that were picking up tar, and a leather purse you bought in Buenos Aires, and you saw the posters and photographs of a triple program with Luis Sandrini, plus *La vuelta de Rocha,* starring Mercedes Simone and Hugo del Carril and you used to enjoy the porteño music of the time, and, in summer, you used to go to outdoor restaurants in Maldonado, Belgrano, in your way to Tigre, in order to listen to Canaro's and Pichuco's orchestras; you were also fond of the music from the interior: the *carnavalito, pericón, vidalita, chacarera*; and they were showing Malambo starring Delia Garcés in another theater and you saw many names and titles you knew for having come here every afternoon since you lived in Buenos Aires, Floren Delbene, Tita Merello, *Tres hombres del río,* Niní Marshall, Esteban Serrador, Santiago Gómez Cou, *Los ojos más lindos del mundo,* Enrique Muiño, Ángel Magaña, the Legrand sisters, *Los martes orquídeas,* Petrone, Amelia Bence, Silvana Roth, *La casa de los millones,* Olinda Bozán, *Semillita...*

"*J'étais une vraie cinglée du cinéma argentin...*"

You finally stopped in front of the photos of *Los muchachos de antes no usaban gomina,* for which you had a passion. You bought your ticket in the box office and went into that small, narrow theater, with tall and uncomfortable wooden seats, where the fans' noise was louder than the sound track and you found a place in the front rows. The film had already begun and the two *1900-pitucos* had gone out partying and had just met the centennial's top prostitute, the *Rubia Mireya,* played by Mecha Ortiz, and the couple was about to dance nothing less than the milonga, "*El cisne*", when you felt somebody was touching your hand and you looked to the right to meet Larraín, the Chilean embassy secretary, who was drinking a *Vascongada* with a straw. He bent to say hello and said the world was rather small, and offered you a sip of his chocolate milk and laughed with a high-pitched sound and said that, just for one afternoon both of you could pretend to be engaged in the theater and that it would be a secret between you ad him, and you wanted to sit, relaxed, bored stiff, watching how the *Rubia Mireya,* dressed as a high courtesan, went down with the inflexible fate of tango to become an old flower seller in the gutter where, of course, she was discovered in the last reel by Arrieta and Parravicini, the aged heartthrobs. A young girl of twenty five summers that won't come back. You thought that tango was one of the few contemporary forms of tragedy and you got up.

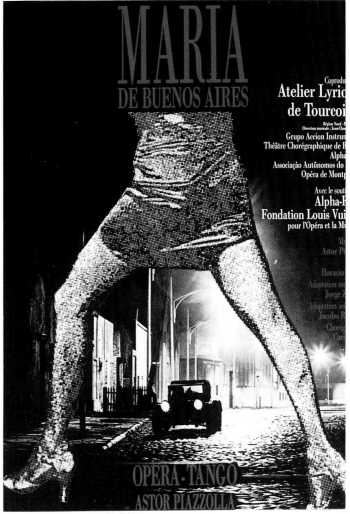

José Sebastián Tallon

"El Cívico" and "La Moreira"

In the years 5, 6, 7 and 8, *"El Cívico"*, who had between twenty five and twenty eight years old, lived in room 15, in *El Sarandí* tenement house (*conventillo*) located in the eponymous street, between Constitución street and Cochabamba. His profession involved exploiting his wife, *"La Moreira"*, as well as fishing and trading, in cash, new young girls. He was of southern Italy descent (albanians); on the other hand, she was a daughter of gypsy andalusians. It is not necessary to describe "El Cívico" as an exceptionally handsome young man, because the essential key to his success, as it is known, was seduction, the indispensable, enchanting seduction of his body. The second key element was his shrewdness —cunning— his disguised criminal coldness, his skill in his handling of the dagger, his courage. (You can clearly see in him the gutsy *compadrito* type.) The third key element was his "warmth", his wealthy-man habits, his fine, very pleasant social manners, his famous skills as a dancer, his gift of the gab. He worshipped everything that was *criollo*. In fact, he was a *criollo* himself and tried being it even more. Out of his own rogue environment, he did not use *caló* terms. (In general, the *caló* and *lunfardo* were less used by the gangsters themselves than by their followers). He called himself an Alem and Yrigoyen supporter, but I never observed, during my expedition to the low districts, an honest political interest. He had a pleasant voice to sing and was a good guitarist.

In the tenement, his room shone as the window of a jewelry store in a dull street. Some Louis XV pieces of furniture, with bows and dolls. Painted cushions by some of his friends in jail. A great number of portraits of him, in which he appeared as a dancer or, decoratively, as a dancer performing a tango step; or with other pimps, in some rural parties. At the head of the bed, the portraits of the parents of "La Moreira" and on the sides, two cards, one for her from Andalusia and one for him, from Ushuaia. On a horsetail, combs and ornamental combs. A big kerose-

Patio in a conventillo.
1907.

ne lamp that was lended by *"El Cívico"* to the neighbors, when there was a party in the patio. Sticking out from the lamp shade, at the end of a metal device that got into the tube in order to protect it, the tenement's children sweetly watched a little tin windmill, that revolved with the heat of the flame. On the visible side of the closet, an expensive guitar which was played by him and by his friends, inside a red velvet case; a peacock and, beneath, the word *Souvenir* had been embroidered on this case, another jail work, no doubt. On the bed, a polychrome blanket from the Pampas which, in addition, he used in the carnivals as part of his brigand fancy dress outfit. On each side of the bed, there was a flowery carpet, and at the head of the bed (at one side, so as not to be hidden by the white tulle mosquito net), a picture of San Roque. Under the pillow, the knife, the dagger or the bayonet (weapon of the *guapos*), reconstructed for his personal use. He allowed his foxterrier, called Pito, to sleep on the blanket. In the toilet, a great collection of make-up and attire accessories, and perfume bottles. (*El Cívico*'s huge and shining quiff was always perfumed, according to the high-class general preference, with *Sola mía*). On the closet mirror, on the upper corners, painted in several colors, a bunch of roses. *"La Moreira"* had covered with an andalusian shawl the back of a rocking chair which *El Cívico* used to have a nap, with his *petit point* moustache support perfectly placed. On a corner cupboard, a musical clock that, before striking the hour, played the opening bars of the National Anthem. On the door and the window, embroidered curtains. On a little table made for that purpose, the *mate* equipment. The silver and gold, three-feet *mate* and *bombilla*. The sugar bowl was, of course, made out of the shell of an armadillo. From the lintel, a small awning hung for the afternoon *mate*. Polite with everybody, *El Cívico* used to seat in the patio, and have mate. Between his fingers decked with jewelry, smoked a *Vuelta abajo, Atorrante or Siglo XX* ci-

garette. The smart girls smiled then, with no danger and flush, behind *La Moreira's* back, casting a glance of glory in his direction, in the presence of his splendid bearing, his attire, his perfume and his long, curled and artistic moustache.

At sunset, *La Moreira* went with others to *La Pichona* café, on Pavón street, between Rincón street and Pasco (a brothel neighborhood), where she "worked" as a prostitute, *lancera*, procuress and dancer. As a *lancera* because she *threw the lance* (the punga) to the alcoholic *jerks* and wealthy *gringos*; as a procuress, because she was her "husband's" partner in the fact of beguiling simple souls and then selling them as "novelties"; as a dancer, because she was, in fact, an extremely good dancer, and because *La Pichona* café was one the places that helped most give tango its well-known fame as a brothel-like dance. By night, she was a tango woman. She carried in her veins the gypsy spirit and, despite having such a feminine look and being so beautiful, in her somber tasks she was very "valuable" as a dagger thrower, from there her surname. She commonly used a knife; but when she had to venture alone in the outer nights or in the hard "businesses" -suffice it to mention the resentment of insignificant, weak, pain in the neck -but no less dangerous- rogues against her, since she took their women away-, she went out wearing knee-high boots and carrying a dagger or a bayonet. You must not forget that the suburbs were experiencing a time of crazy lust and violence. Her figure: not very tall, a perfect figure, a sensual voice and face; and deportment; an olive-colored complexion, jet black hair and eyes, an eager nose, small mouth, excellent bust. Silk blue or red robe with white spots. Sometimes, a fancy tartan or flowery *pompadour*, long-sleeved dressing gown with lace cuffs. She fastened her robe, from the throat to the breasts, with a silk cordon, zigzagging through the embroidered buttonholes, finished off with a bow and tassels. The lace, stiff collar, surrounding her neck, showed a lace edging. She wore a corset that strongly hugged her waist and was tightened by stays; a gray or light green pleated and very full

Sigfredo Pastor: El Cívico y La Moreira, *xylography.*

skirt with the *frou-frou* of the starchy petticoat or taffeta. *"Rosa de Francia"*, *"Agua Florida"*, "Jour de gloire" perfumes. She wore her hair in a bun, with shell bobby pins and back combs, big gold earrings -as large as the rim of a glass-, and the necklace with a photo frame. Well, *"El Cívico's"* portrait was in that photo frame.

He also went out at sunset, but a while later. Before taking a car on Entre Ríos Avenue, he used to kill time at Rucha's restaurant, on San Juan street, between Sarandí street and Rincón, a night shelter for scoundrels, the artists from the Corrado Circus, traveling country singers, musicians. Later, at the corner of Entre Ríos Avenue and San Juan, he would accept the invitation of a friend or colleague for a *suiset* at the Café Pagés. Finally, he would take a carriage that would leave him at *Hansen's,* in Palermo, or near any bar of La Boca, if he had no "business" on the clandestine side relating to María La Vasca (at the corner of Carlos Calvo street and Jujuy), or Laura (at the corner of Paraguay street and Pueyrredón), or at some "commission agent's" home. He had a preference for Hansen's, because every *compadrito* of his kind always yearned to rub shoulders with people in high circles.

He had a square hair cut and wore a black, gray or flea-colored hat at a tilt over the ear; an open, low collar, and a cravat with a pearl or diamonds. Starched dicky and detachable cuffs, rose or light blue on cream background. Lavish gold cuff links with his initials. The black or blue, or gray, or tartan-like double-breasted jacket was rather short, with high shoulder reinforcements. Wide lapels, closed over the cravat, with satin facings (if the jacket was black) or trimmed with silk braids. The colored jackets had six nacre buttons and, between the two short back slits — they were called *culero* jackets— there were another three nacre buttons on each side. The vest was fastened and could be made of white piqué or fancy thick satin. A heavy gold chain hung from the chest pockets and was tied to the first buttonhole, from which a sterling gold medallion glittered. The tight French-style plain or checkered trousers,

with a very high waist and adjusted to the ankle boot's or boot's instep, with three nacre buttons in the cuffs. (Carefully arranged and sheathed, *El Cívico's* bayonet was placed vertically on the side of his right thigh.) The ankle boot or the boot were made of shining lambskin. The high heel, called "pear heel", was shaped to a point with the size of a twenty cent coin. The boots were so fine and soft that you could fold them and put them in your pocket. And finally, besides wearing the *jailaife* latest styles (in tango slang, the *jailaife* was the one who dressed well; it was a word coming from the english term *high life*), *El Cívico*, as the famous tango composer, Arolas, liked to wear rings over the gloves and a little vicuña poncho around his shoulders.

As you can see, the *compadritos* used to exaggerate in the way they dressed up. They exaggerated everything. The term relaxed was used at the time to define them. Those who got to such a point that they wore rings over their gloves were called "loose guys" by the *compadritos* themselves. They copied wealthy people's fashion, and they dressed up with a feminine exaggerated, clearly sexual and suspicious narcissism; they took tango and led it to obscene sexual milieus. The creole swinging of the hips, caused by the high-heeled shoes, was changed into a somewhat silly, if not effeminate, walk. By the same token, they gave tango choreography their own style, with erotic exaggerations.

Everything in *El Cívico*, as in his equals, was erotic. Sexuality was for him a passionate and exclusive calling. He was a lover and pornomaniac —allow me the explosion of this neologism— by temperament. He was a dealer by trade, something that vegetatively grew from his congenital individualism. But I want to refer not only to the internal psychic characters, but to his biological individuality as well. In fact, I want to talk about his appearance. If the appearance of a well differentiated and honest man does not show any sign of erotism, not even in his private life, in the

The flirtatious comment and the smile, Circa 1900.

pimp I'm referring to, there were signs of it everywhere. From the hair perfume to the shoe shine, everything in him was erotic. And from his eyes to his way of walking, from his affected language to the jewelry he wore on his refined hands. And he loved his woman that way. But what really appalled you about this conceited character who called himself a sterling *criollo* —and, in that way, he was not different from his colleagues— was the love for his wife. *El Cívico* loved that professional prostitute who kissed him good-bye every day at sunset to go to the brothel. *La Moreira* was really his sweetheart, his partner forever. And he loved her without intervals, with a careful and full-time commitment. He besieged her. His political indifference —among many others— testified to this obsessive continuity, the concentration of his conscience on the love concern. The permanence of this union did not depend, in his case, on the marriage contract, but on his ghoulish love capacity, his ever-changing appeal of a consummate artist of sex. With no bourgeois habits, with no distractions, with no physical or mental absences, in his private life he was all refined, constant caress for the even sensitivity of his wife, and he knew how to bewitch her even while she was sleeping. When he hit her, she just took it, even if she was able to fight with him on equal terms, because he wouldn't punish her with the same brutality as those who had no better way of controlling their prostitutes than making demands as a handsome owner or a jealous lover. If she had left him, he would have killed her; or perhaps, he would have drank his troubles away and, finally died of sorrow, for her. Since Contursi, the Argentine people have always been moved by the complaints of the abandoned *canflinflero*.

Manuel Gálvez

A suburban story

Carnival arrived. For Rosalinda it was a sad time because Daniel's mother was taken seriously ill. In the neighborhood, a carnival parade was organized, and groups of masked people in fancy dress walked in the streets. The tenement's girls had fun at the parties of the recreational associations, and even Saturnina, wearing ridiculous clothes and plastering her face with vulgar face powder, took a stroll with a character who, according to what was said in the house, was her lover.

One afternoon, Rosalinda was called by Daniel to the room where he lived with his mother so that she could know her and accompany her. The sick woman was very pleased her son had such a nice and beautiful girlfriend. Rosalinda was impressed by that room, that home. The place was all cleanliness, order, affection, contrasting with her house where at every corner, dirt, vice, disorder and hate appeared. Oh! How happy she would be if only she could leave Saturnina and come to such a nice and decent home! But, would that ever happen?

One night, on the eve of the octave, several masked persons showed up at the tenement house. Among them, there was a *gaucho* who played the guitar and another one who played the accordion. Everyone in the house went to the long courtyard where all the rooms looked onto. There were about ten single and married women, and the dance started at once.

Linda stood watching from her room's door. She did not want to dance, since she was seeing somebody and feeling so sad. She thought about Daniel and his ill mother, even if she was better now.

In the meantime, from the guitar and the bandoneon, some compadron tango phrases emerged. It was a sensual, mean, suburban music, a mixture of insolence and lowness, stiffness and voluptuousness, age-old sadness and the coarse joy of a brothel, a music that spoke in a passionate criminal slang, and recalled scenes of a bad life, in rough areas full of criminal silhouettes. The melody showed variable lines, one moment a united tune and the next a divided one, one moment a straight melody and the next a winding one. It became somewhat rigid to break at once. Sometimes it

rushed only to stop suddenly; or it beat rhythmic and hard punches only to slip away towards the end.

Everybody danced in the yard under its soporific and disquieting charm, and its taste which, as a strong wine, made people feel light-headed and lose their senses. The couples drifted slowly across the yard. They went up and down, they twisted from one side to another, they kept walking stiffly and straight and, finally, they stopped to rock themselves forward and backward, as grotesque silhouettes, each man stuck to his woman: the latter showed gravity, with half-closed eyes, and the men, a baleful look under their wide-brimmed hats right over their eyes.

Linda smiled while she looked at some couples —at Saturnina who was held by a count full of feathers, and at the tenement's manager, a genovese woman round as a ball who jumped up and down in the arms of a fierce Moreira— when she was suddenly thunderstruck: in front of her, "El Chino" had appeared. He had grown up and had a scar on his chin. Linda felt she was pierced by the malevo's eyes and, suddenly, the last months, the beautiful memories, her love, vanished into thin air. She forgot absolutely everything. The only thing she was aware of was that that man had made her his and controlled her and that she was forced to obey him. Enveloped in *El Chino's* arms, she left herself be carried to the middle of the patio and danced and danced for a long time, mechanically, without knowing what she was doing or why she was doing it.

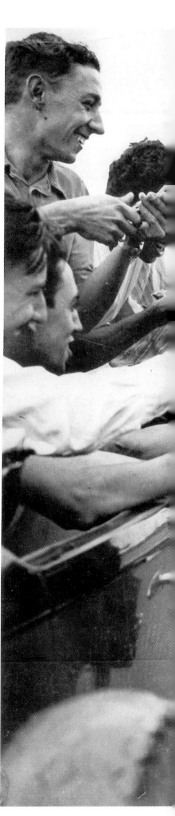

Carnival on the Costanera Avenue. 1935.

The carnival parade goes on

Tell me who you are
tell me where you go
cheerful little masked person
who shouts at me:
"How are you...? Do you know me...?
Bye...Bye...Bye...
I'm the mysterious little woman
you're looking for!"

Lyrics by Francisco García Jiménez
Music by Anselmo Aieta

49

Alberto Vacarezza

Your cradle was a tenement house

A tenement's patio in Villa Crespo. Lateral doors and street towards the back. (It is five p.m. The audience's right and left). The "Chino" Rancagua. "El Palomo". Don Julián. Samuel. Rosita. First Percanta, second Percanta. A Suitor and Neighbors. (When the curtain goes up, the "chino" Rancagua sings to the sound of his guitar. Don Antonio, "El Palomo", Don Julián and Samuel are listening to him. Rosita prepares a mate for Don Julián. Both Percantas are at the entrance door, chatting with the Suitor.)

RANCAGUA: —My old friend, man
has been made to suffer...
And this is the opportunity
for men to show their strength...
Till death comes
And takes them away smacking their heads
around..."
D. JULIÁN *(Excited)*: —Very good, my friend...! That's singing. I don't want these imported guys saying that the only thing we have here is cereals and cattle.
EL PALOMO: —Are you comparing these howls with a song of my land?
D.ANTONIO: —And are you trying to say that your Spanish thing can be compared to the Italian song?
EL PALOMO: —And since when do you think you are above everyone else? Do you really know what the *cante jondo* is? Have you ever heard in a starry night the moan of a *malagueña* that squeezes your heart and leaves it as small as a hazelnut?
D.ANTONIO: —Come on, don't talk nonsense, you spanish maximalist! Do you know what's inside a *tarantela*?
EL PALOMO: —And have you ever heard a *sevillana*...?
D.ANTONIO: —Do you know the *Luchía de la Marmota*'s romance?
EL PALOMO: —And do you know what a *granaína* is?
D.ANTONIO: —Yes sir. I like *granadina* very much, but with soda...
SAMUEL: —But what are you talking about! If you knew the israelite song, you wouldn't talk like that!
D.JULIÁN: —Another one who talks to himself...! And what does all that mean compared

The inside of two late 19th-century tenement houses.

to one of our styles, a *vidalita, cueca, malambo, firmeza*...?
RANCAGUA: —And tango, where do you leave it? Where do you leave tango, with its sweet, grumpy and harmonious notes...?
D.ANTONIO: —Don't talk to me about tango, *per la madona*...! What is tango...? It's nothing but *caran can cangue*...! "Throw me the chest", "Follow me as you think best..." "Move over if you don't want to be run over by a car..." and you never get out of there...! But what do you mean with tango? Would you analyze it for me...?
RANCAGUA *(He suddenly gets angry, throws his hat away and makes himself comfortable.)*: —Listen, buddy: Tango,
using Bettinoti's and Gabino's
sweet language,
is joy and sadness,
it's love, hate, treason,
it's weakness and strength...!
The shouts of the lout
who swears to get his eternal revenge
when the chick stood him up;
and it's her moans
when she cries in the flophouse
full of nostalgia for the absence.
It's the girls' laugh
and the old women's anger.
It's the reconnaissance round,
that there, in the fateful night
is carried out by the half asleep cop
on the threshold of a door...
Bugle call!
Chime of the bells...!
And finally, my dear blockhead,
so that you can understand me better:
It's the complaints of the dandy
who gets to the apartment,
seriously wounded, because a while ago
he was given a severe beating.
It's the mother's kisses
when her son has been arrested,
and the joy of the man who's coming back
after a long time in prison,
and at the flophouse finds,
with open arms,
the sweet chick waiting for him...
(The Percantas come back from the front door and walk silently away through the corridors, right and left.)

León Benarós

Hansen & company

Hansen is the most important and lasting myth among the *porteño* places related to tango. Around it, there were other places where people used to dance: *El Tambo* or *Tambito*, *El Velódromo*, the *Pabellón de los Lagos*, a not very coherent "complex" which we are going to call "Hansen and company".

When was *Hansen* inaugurated? When did it close? Which was its exact location? Who was its first licensee? Who did exploit the establishment throughout its existence? Did people dance at *Hansen* or not? Which was the character, the aspect, the atmosphere of this famous and almost mythological place of tango?

Not all these questions have been answered accurately, with the same criteria, by different researchers. Anyway, *Hansen* was not strictly called *Hansen* but "Restaurant 3 de Febrero", a name that appeared in the papers but was not used by people. Vicente Cutolo, on gathering different kinds of information from Ricardo N. Llanes, Jorge Alberto Bossio and Mario A. Mabragaña, makes a summary in his *Nuevo Diccionario Biográfico Argentino* where he mentions the first licensee, Juan Hansen: "He was of German, not Swedish origin, as it has been generally said. He was a licensee of the famous restaurant located in the district of Palermo that was opened on November 11, 1875. It was located at the corner of Sarmiento Avenue and Casares Avenue (today, Figueroa Alcorta Avenue), at the side of the Argentine Central Railroad, on a site that was transferred by the State. It looked like an old rural house and at the front, the following sign stood for many years: *Restaurant del Parque 3 de Febrero* and J. Hansen. In the daytime, the families who were strolling around the park used to go there to have a snack or a beer. By contrast, at night, always very lively, it was profusely illuminated. From several blocks, you could discover its location following the carriages' lights and the lamps that lit up the arbors. You could have dinner there, in the midst of laughs and chat and, in the large courtyard, the patrons would have a drink under the leafy and fragrant wisterias and honeysuckles. A number of selected ensembles provided the music for the meeting, playing milongas, polcas and waltzes. Until 11 p.m., it was a peaceful restau-

The Pabellón de los Lagos, and the restaurant at the 3 de Febrero Park, J. Hansen. c.1900.

rant, but as from that time, the place was frequented by night strollers, *guapos* and tough gangs who made it very popular. *Hansen* died in Buenos Aires on April 3, 1892, at the age of 58. He married *doña* Ana Anderson. The only reason why his name was incorporated into the history of tango is that the establishment that had him as its first licensee, kept his name until it reached its splendor, managed by different licensees, with the parties that were given there with a genuine *compadre* touch. It was pulled down in 1912, during Dr. Joaquín S. de Anchorena municipal administration. At the turn of the century, *Hansen's*, thanks to its fame and prestige, turned into a legendary place."

Cutolo holds that at *"Hansen"* there were *"parties of a genuine* compadre *touch"*. That's the widespread legend which, since it is sentimentally pleasant, we do not want to leave aside. Some other statements, however, say that at Hansen people did not dance. They only went to listen to music —including tangos— and to have a beer or dinner.

On December 16, 1961, we interviewed Felipe Amadeo Lastra, already an octogenarian, at his home address, at 2009, J. A. Pacheco de Melo street, second floor, apartment 5 (he later moved to Quintana Avenue). We had been introduced to him by our beloved and admired Justo P. Sáenz (Jr.), the greatest expert at creole things we have ever met, who provided us with an honest, accurate and photographic information. Amadeo Lastra —old breeder of creole horses— had also been a "young stroller" as many others. He showed us a photo of him, at *Hansen*, with Ricardo Güiraldes, we did not dare to require. He told us very interesting things about the old Buenos Aires. We urged him to write. He told us he could not write and we suggested he should do it without literary hopes, accumulating as many data as possible. He finally gave us the original text of *Recuerdos del 900* that we have published with our own prologue.

Amadeo Lastra vehemently insisted on the fact that *"at* Hansen *people didn't dance"*. *"Where do you think they could dance? Among the trees?"* he said in explanation of his remark.

As an habitué of *Hansen's* he gave us a valuable description: *"It was located on the Avenida de las Palmeras, as soon you crossed the Railroad. It faced north towards San Isidro. It was like an old rural house. It had a large, outdoor courtyard, with a black and white tiled floor, I believe, surrounded by wooden kiosks made up of wickerwork grilles painted green, embracing the kitchen with its larder. Hansen was a restaurant. We used to go there after midnight. The mosquitoes were a real pest. There were no women there. We had to take them with us. The women led the way, the men followed. In former times"*, added Amadeo Lastra, "Hansen" was called "Café Tarana". *In 1900 it was still called Hansen. I have a photo of the place dated back to 1900. I believe it was closed around 1911."*

In 1952, we interviewed Roberto Firpo, who played at Hansen. He categorically confirmed that people did not dance at Hansen. He recognized that some couples could have danced sporadically in a bower. *"I played"*, told us Firpo whom we interviewed at his apartment on Callao avenue, *"at Hansen in 1908. I signed up for two pesos. It was an old building. Meals were served outdoors, in the bowers. But people mostly had a drink. The patrons were elegant, wealthy people. Some people say that people used to dance there. It's not true. Music was played to be listened to. Perhaps one or two couples sporadically danced in a small bower. There were several bowers. Each woman came with her partner. Some men went even with three women. Many used to celebrate at Hansen their graduation and performed true humorous pantomimes. Someone shouted: 'Che, ring the bell! I have to get to the ambulance!' Another one acted as a drunk. They talked about the operations they had performed. Almost all of them were handsome boys. A young doctor from the Salaberry Hospital, named Massolo, I believe, also used to go there. Many of them belonged to the Posses gang. They knew how to box and they later learned jiu-jitsu. No matter how thin some of them were, they would knock down compadritos armed with a dagger. I worked there when a licensee, Giardini Payot, took charge of the place."*

Sigfredo Pastor: Jorge Newbery
dancing tango, *oil painting.*

In 1951, we interviewed Luis Teisseire, the author of *Entrada Prohibida*, who knew *Hansen* and played there his tango, *La Nación*, for the first time. He told us about Anselmo Tarana, the new licensee. He gave the place his name —*Café Tarana*— but he added a phrase as an aide-mémoire: Antiguo *Hansen*. *"Tarana,"* said Teisseire, *"introduced a change: an old bus fetched the customers at Palermo's gates. He was an elegant Italian, —perhaps from Rome or Tuscany—with special poise, who used to wear a top hat. He had an impressive appearance. He had been a lessee in the Cacheuta thermal facilities. He was shot by a girl's father. He was caught in bed with his own niece."*

What can be added about *El Velódromo, El Tambito, el Pabellón de los Lagos*? In 1952, Roberto Firpo said: *"I began at* El Velódromo *with the piano, in 1907, with Bevilacqua. By then, I was twenty two years old and I came from* Los Corrales, *on Rioja street and Caseros. The owner was Pesce who I believe was the father of the person who was later the owner of the Luna Park.* El Velódromo *took up four enclosed blocks. In the middle of the place there was an embankment. Inside, there was a track where the cyclists used to ride. You got there through a dirt track that sometimes was a quagmire. It was located two blocks from* Hansen. *Drinks were served on little tin tables, under the trees. It also had some rooms. From* El Velódromo, *you could see when someone was playing at* Hansen. *The* Gaucha Manuela *used to go there; she was a young man's kept woman who was said to have eaten up four or five million. She was a very beautiful dark-haired girl, with a very creole way of speaking. She was quite capable of taking a knife and hitting. I dedicated a tango to her:* La Gaucha Manuela. *We were often asked to dedicate our music, and, sometimes, we received one hundred pesos for it. I dedicated that tango 'to the distinguished Miss Manuela López. At* El Velódromo *I earned one peso a day and some tips. There were no women. Each man brought his own."*

El Tambo, also called *El Tambito*, was a real milking yard during some hours of the day, but in the afternoon, it was like a café where you could have a snack. It was near *El Velódromo,* close to Vieytes Avenue, at the other side of the railroad with regard to *El Velódromo.* Said Roberto Firpo: "It was a real milking yard. There were some dairy cows. The owner was a thin, tall, elegant and communicative spaniard. His wife was a stout, dark-haired spanish woman. There were small tables under the trees. There was a shelf with drinks. Sometimes, there was not even light at *El Tambito.* It was located in the neighborhood of Palermo, in a place where long time ago, the bicycles were put away. It had no fences. I believe that's where a young Argerich got killed. At *El Tambito,* people used to create a huge ruckus."

El *Pabellón de los Lagos* had an ostentatious entry as that of a mosque with its minaret, a sort of globular coupole, very typical of the "turn-of-the-century" style.

In 1912, an old member of the Jockey Club, José Castaños, told us, *"the only night place for general relaxation was the* Pabellón de los Lagos. *It was located in the neighborhood of Palermo, where you can find now the Andalusean Patio. It had boxes, with privets at the back. The place lasted until 1913 or 1914.* Hansen *disappeared before that, when the Argentine Central Railroad and the Buenos Aires-Rosario Railroad merged, and the railroad tracks were removed."*

Hansen's legend! A careful research gradually destroys a story of guapos and *compadritos* that was not very plausible. First, due to economic reasons: borderline people could not go to *Hansen's* because it was an expensive place. Second, it seems that the police security was rather strict. Perhaps the fact of staring at someone else's woman or launching an olive to a neighboring table could have caused a storm. But a storm that used to break among the young regular patrons. Even so, the appearance of a wealthy pimp at *Hansen's* should be regarded as a possibility in the same way that the "well-to-do young men" used to get into the tough

suburban area with the intention of acting as good family *guapos*...

Hansen, the famous establishment with an ambiguous look, somewhere between a viennese café and an old rural estate, with its night neighboring cafés, is part, however, of the undestructible fable which no disappointing research can fight against, or deny the danced presence of tango...

References

Locations in the Gardens of Palermo, according an old map by Pablo Ludwing, published in 1891:
1. General Belgrano Railway.- 2. General San Martín Railway.- 3. General Mitre Railway.- 4. Municipal Planetary.- 5. Sarmiento Avenue.- 6. Café de Hansen.- 7. Velodrome.- 8. Monument to Urquiza.- 9. The Kiosquito.- 10. The Tambito Café, former Kiosco Casares.- 11. Power station.- 12. Pabellón de los Lagos.- 13. Manuelita Rosas' Aromo del Perdón.- 14. Libertador Avenue.- 15. Monument to the Carta Magna. Today, Monument to The Spaniards.- 16. Zoo.- 17. Figueroa Alcorta Avenue.

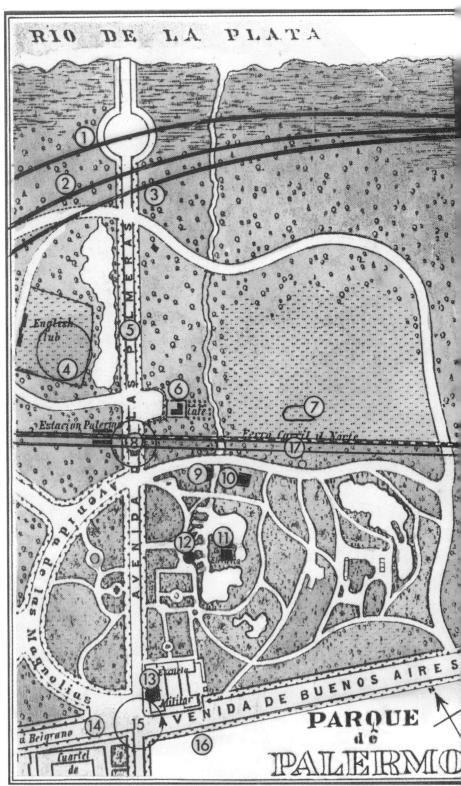

The Palermo Station of the Northern Railway.
1881. Today, in the place which was occupied by
Hansen.

Page 58. *Florida Street: the faces of Buenos Aires.*

Palermo forest.

Bandoneón soul

Meaning and emotion

Jorge Luis Borges

Tango

Where may they be? asks the elegy
About those who are not anymore,
          as if there were
A region where Yesterday could
Be Now, Still and Yet.

Where may the malevos be (I repeat)
those who founded, in dusty, dirt alleys
Or in dead-end towns,
The knife and courage sect?

Where may those who have gone be
Leaving an episode to the epic,
A fable to time, and who with no hate,
Profit or love passion in mind,
          stabbed each other?

I look for them in their legend, in the last
Ember that, like a vague rose,
Keeps some of that brave rabble
From Los Corrales and Balvanera.

In what dark alleys or barren land
From the next world will the tough
Shadow of a man who was a dark shadow,
Muraña, that knife of Palermo, live?

And that fatal Iberra (may the saints
Have mercy on him) who on a railroad bridge,
Killed his brother, "El Ñato",
          who had to answer for
More deaths than himself, and in doing so,
          reached his score?

A mythology of knives
Slowly sinks into oblivion;
A chanson de geste has been lost
Among sordid police news.

There is another ember, another burning rose
From the ashes that keep them in one piece;
That's where the superb brawlers
and the weight of the quiet dagger lie.

Even if the hostile dagger or that
          other dagger,
Time, have lost them in mud,
Today, beyond time and the fateful
Death, these dead men live in tango.

They are in the music, in the strings
Of the stubborn, laborious guitar,
That weaves in the happy *milonga*
The party and innocence of courage.

The yellow wheel of horses and lions,
turns around, and I hear the echo
of those tangos by Arolas and Greco
that were danced on the sidewalks.

At a moment which today emerges as isolated,
Without a before or an after, against oblivion,
And has the taste of what is lost,
What is lost and recovered.

There are old things in the chords:
The other courtyard and the made out vine.
(Behind the distrustful walls
The South keeps a dagger and a guitar.)

That gust, tango, that wonder,
defies the busy years;
Made of dust and time, man lasts
Less than the light melody,

That is only time. Tango creates a shady
Unreal past that is somehow true.
A memory which has hardly died
Fighting, on a suburban corner.

Drawing of a compadrito, *by Jorge Luis Borges that was on show at the Primer Salón de Escritores. 1926.*

Boats and ships in La Boca of the Riachuelo.

Victoria Ocampo

My Vision about Tango

Palais de Glace

1920-Palé de Glas,
you don't exist
anymore
with your warm atmosphere...
I danced there
my student tangos,
I dreamt there
about the guys of the past...

Lyrics and music by Enrique Cadícamo

And what about tango? Tango which is today so patriotically extolled we cannot turn on the faucet of the radio or TV without hearing a flow of this music you can dance to.

At the beginning, what I got from tango was sifted, as many other things. I was not attracted by its ever-plaintive melody and its slow, dragged rhythm. Much less by the blubbering emphasis and cheap sentimentalism of its lyrics. I have only liked it, a lot, when I began to dance it. As a dance, I discovered its inimitably argentine character. In its best and worst sense. But it took me some time to know it under this aspect. Tango was not danced in the porteño ballrooms or among the adolescents of today's vilified class. I saw it danced for the first time (Oh! What a desecration!) at my grandfather's (the one of the mate), on Lavalle 777 (today, the Ambassador theater). The big, rambling house with patios and magnolias at the back, was periodically invaded by 32 turbulent grandsons of different ages. This, fortunately, enabled the children to be divided into different groups (those who were over fifteen, and those who were under fifteen) and once a week, one of these groups would go to lunch or dinner with their grandparents. The older grandson began to date with somebody. He was a great tango dancer, out of his parents' house, and, one day, after he had taken all the necessary precautions with the intention of not being "caught", we were dazzled by him, when he and his girlfriend displayed their tango dancing skill. We confined ourselves in a small parlor of the old house (currently the center of the Ambassador theater) which was not frequented by grownups. The couple (they were magnificent examples of youth beauty) danced cheek to cheek amid an almost religious silence. That was my first vision of tango and I did not understand why such a solemn dance had been forbidden.

Some years later, every Thursday, no matter what, the Pibe de la Paternal (Fresedo) would come to my house followed by his companions. Tango was danced the whole afternoon. The champions of these memorable days were Ricardo Güiraldes (with no more fame than that we, his friends, suspected he would earn some day) and Vicente Madero.

Bailarines, *drawing by Raúl Soldi.*

The latter's talent bordered on genius, and I believe nobody ever had been able to surpass him. When he walked tango, his whole body, looking still, flexibly followed the rhythm, he experienced it and communicated it to his partner who, infected by it, obeyed that perfect and rhythmic gait. The dramatically schmaltzy words of those tangos were hardly important. They were redeemed by dancers as perfect as Vicente and Ricardo.

Percanta who caught me...
Romantic little apartment...
etc., etc., etc.

We were young and words such as faded and worn out could apply neither to our unwrinkled faces nor to our agile and tireless bodies. From Paris, Ricardo Güiraldes wrote to me: "In all fairness, I've been well received at Mrs. Bulteau's (a lady who had a well-known literary group) and I've been introduced to nice people, but those wednesdays were not as good as the previous thursdays... Youth! Beauty! Eternal springboard to the ideal (see my Salomé from the *Cencerro de Cristal* or other digressions)."

That's what tango was for me. And I don't care that for some people that's not true tango. It was mine.

The Osvaldo Fresedo orchestra. 1920s.

Social gathering at the Palais the Glace. 1916.

Ernesto Sabato

Metaphysics of tango

In this country of opponents, each time one does something (prepares a budget, writes a symphony or makes a housing plan), thousands of critics emerge at once and demolish it with a sadistic meticulousness.

One of the declarations of this inferiority feeling of the argentinos (who takes pleasure in destroying that which he does not feel capable of doing) is the doctrine that discredits the literature with a metaphysic stress: it says it is foreign to our reality, imported and apocryphal and, finally, that it is a characteristic of the european decadence.

According to this peculiar doctrine, the "metaphysical illness" can only affect the people who live in Paris or Rome. And, if one takes into account that this metaphysical illness is the result of man's finite nature, one must conclude that for these theorists, people only die in Europe.

One must explain to these people, who not only refuse to consider their shortsightedness as a drawback but, on the contrary, they use it as an instrument of their research, that if the metaphysical illness torments a european, an argentinian should feel tormented twice over, since if man is transitory in Rome, he is much more transient here, as we have a feeling we are living this transitory existence in a camp and in the middle of a universal cataclysm, without that support from eternity that is a thousand-year-old tradition.

This is true to such a point that even tango authors make metaphysics without knowing it.

Because for the said critics, metaphysics can only be found in huge and dark treaties by german professors; but the fact is that it is found, as Nietzsche said, in the middle of the street, in the human tribulations of common human beings.

This is not the place to discuss how the metaphysical concern constitutes the subject-matter of our best literature. We just want to emphasize it, in this humble suburb of the argentine literature called tango.

Buenos Aires' violent and tumultuous growth, the arrival of millions of hopeful hu-

man beings and their almost constant frustration, nostalgia for the distant homeland, the natives' resentment against the invasion, the feelings of insecurity and frailty in a world that was increasingly changing, the fact that people couldn't find a safe meaning of the existence, the lack of absolute hierarchies, everything manifests itself in the metaphysics of tango.

It melancholically says:
It erased the asphalt with one swipe,
the old neighborhood where I was born...

Progress that was imposed with their hammers by the rulers of the new Argentina razed the country to the ground. In fact, not one brick survived, a material which is more ephemeral and, as a result, philosophically more distressing.

Nothing remains in the ghost town.

And the popular poet sings his nostalgia for the old *"Café de los Angelitos"*:
I recall you, lost in life
and tangled up in the threads of smoke.

And, as a modest suburban Manrique, he asks himself:
Which dreams did they run after?...
Which stars have they gone to?
The voices that arrived,
and passed and kept quiet yesterday,
where are they?,
through which streets will they come back?

The *porteño*, as no one in Europe, feels that Time goes by and that the frustration of all his dreams and final death are his inevitable epilogues. And leaned on the little marble table, with some glasses of *semillón* and black tobacco cigarettes, meditative and friendly, he asks:
Remember, brother, the old times?
Or with a cynical bitterness he states:
Life slips away, it slips away and does
not come back.
The best we can do is to enjoy it and pack
in our sorrows.

64

Discepolín, like Horace, sees the woman he once loved as old, faded and worn out. In the existentialist lyrics of his greatest tangos, he says:

When you realize that next to you
they are trying on the clothes
you'll leave behind...
you'll remember this fool
who one day, tired,
began to bark!

The tango man is a profound human being who meditates about the passage of time and about what that passage finally brings us: the inexorable death.

That way, an almost unknown lyricist gloomily whispers:

Tonight, my heroic deeds
have ended forever.
Mysterious words
are cornering my heart...

And ends up saying, with the sinister arrogance of a lonely porteño:

I want to die with myself,
with no confession and no God
crucified to my sorrow,
as clinging to a rancor.

Carlos Alonso: El bandoneonista, *oil painting.*

Page 66: View of Barracas, late-19th century.

Eladia Blázquez

The south-facing
heart

I was born in a neighborhood where luxury was a risk,
that's why my heart is facing south.
My old man was a bee in the beehive,
with clean hands, and a good soul...
And in that childhood temperance forged me,
later, life paved me a thousand ways,
and I learned about the magnate and the gambler,
that's why my heart is facing south.

My neighborhood was a jasmine plant,
the shadow of my mother in the garden,
the sweet party of the simplest things
and the peaceful lawn facing the sun.
My neighborhood was my people who are not there,
the things that will never come back,
from the day I left
with my emotions and my cross
I know that my heart is looking south!

I have my neighborhood's geography on me,
that's why maybe I didn't entirely leave:
the corner, the grocery store, the children
I recognize them... they are a part of me...
Now I know that distance is not real
and I discover myself in that cardinal point,
returning to childhood from light,
always keeping my heart facing south.

Horacio Salas

My poor dear mother

*"I'm called the Poor Little Old Woman",
grumbled the woman with sparkling, bewitching
eyes, "or the Little Good Mother. I lived in lousy,
unventilated tango verses. Which was my profession? That of supporting a group of bums who
slept on their beds or learned to play some bandoneons as wretched as my life. And, of course,
they kept asking for mate at the top of their
lungs, at any time of the day or night! And I kept
rushing around, poor old woman!, from the burner to the bed, and from the bed to the burner."*
Leopoldo Marechal *(Megafón)*

In a short poem he once read in a radio
program as a gloss for Los Chalchaleros and
that was not included in any book, Jaime Dáva-
los condenses: *Land of* Conquistadores */ it has
always been a land of gauchos. / Those smart, /
quarrelsome and singer gauchos, / who, hardened to the rigors of life / and with no dogs bar-
king at them, / no God, law or father, / never
could believe / in a woman's love/ except for
their mother's.* The *conquistador* could hardly
settle, because he was, in essence, an adventu-
rous nomad. Behind him, he left abandoned
women and children who would only know
their mothers. It only seems natural that, under these circumstances, America should
emerge as a bastard continent.

Well into the 19th century, the women of
the argentine countryside, except for some
tasks –such as shearing, for example– were
seen as a necessary but useless element. The
sexual urges were solved either through (legal or illegal) brothels located near the pulpe-
rías (old taverns), or by itinerant groups of
prostitutes who traveled in huge carts, led by
a madam who managed them.

Historian Richard W. Slatta explains that
the *estancieros* (local ranchers) agreed with
Carlos Pellegrini's sentence according to
which, the presence of women in the countryside was forbidden because they were the cause of disputes among the rural workers. At the
turn of the century, Miguel A. Lima reaffirms
this stance saying that they gave way to disorder and provoked fights, and that it was advi-
sable to allow only foremen's and settlers' families. The american researcher adds that the
elite's attitude stressed that, in the countrysi-

de, efficiency and order were before any other
consideration, and he concludes: *"Many* estancieros *only hired single rural workers, or forced
the married ones to leave their families elsewhe-
re during the working season."*

At the turn of the century, when women
and children proved to be efficient in farm
works, the landowners gradually accepted the
settlement of rural families. In addition, the
women, given the shortage of doctors, acted
as folk healers and midwives, others worked
as maids at the landowner's house, or tried to
emigrate to the cities with the purpose of
doing housework.

On the outskirts of the cities —as it has already been said— *guapos* and *compadres* sel-
dom married, as they were aware how risky
their lives were. The first mistake with the
knife or a cunning shot could easily end their
activities as bodyguards of some politician
and even their very existence. For the rest,
the low wages for temporary jobs did not en-
courage marriage either. On the other hand,
the structure of immigration, mostly made up
of single or married men who traveled alone
with the intention of getting a good job and later calling the family that had been left in the
village, did not make it easy to form strong
and firm family unions.

According to the statistics from the Direc-
ción General de Inmigración, between 1857
and 1924, 70% of those who arrived in the
country were men. President Sarmiento had
already expressed his concern when he realized that *"there were only a few women and children among the immigrants."*

Under these circumstances, to which we
have to add the abandonment of their occasio-
nal partners when they realized that, in extreme poverty or misery, they would have to take charge of an extra mouth to feed, the number of sons registered as "of unknown father"
was very important. On the other hand, preg-
nancies, due to a complete lack of knowledge
regarding sexual physiology and efficient con-
traceptives, resulted from sporadic relationships, and men refused to be tied down by a
temporary attraction.

The tango man, son of a bastard class and
a bastard himself (Gardel, the archetype, was

LAGRIMAS

TANGO SENTIMENTAL

POR EDUARDO AROLAS

: TALLERES GRAFICOS MUSICALES :
— FRANCISCO DE PAULA —
· BRASIL 1190 :: M. DE OCA 1683 ·

3ª EDICION

not a bastard by chance), not only lacks lineage but family, and centers all of his primary affections on his mother. The father is an absence, a nonexistent figure that can be replaced, for example, by the admiration for a political leader who plays the role of a father in a collective way or for the neighborhood's *guapo*, another protector, or for any other character who, for different reasons, will influence the orphan or be an example for him. The fact that the two greatest 20th-century mass leaders, Hipólito Yirigoyen, who was mainly followed by the petite bourgeoisie, and Juan Domingo Perón who became a leader for those who lived in the industrial area and the workers coming from the interior within the framework of the 1930s and early-1940s rural exodus, have played, thirty years apart, the same role as "father of the poor" or "father of the needy", is not a coincidence. The biological father has been replaced by a leader who is loved and idealized, who makes no mistakes, exactly the way children see their own fathers in the first years.

In *Juan Nadie*, Miguel D. Etchebarne summarizes the situation of a typical tango man on starting his compadre's biography:

> The mother, as a slave
> yielded under the yoke:
> somebody got everything from her
> and on top of that, beat her.
> (The father, of brave lineage,
> died when Juan was born,
> and not even in a photograph
> could he give a glimpse to his face,
> but he felt his presence,
> sometimes, when he suffered.)

As it seems natural, the tangos, as soon as they began to include lyrics, reflected this reality: mothers who played the double father-mother role, mothers-saints to whom it is always possible to come back in search of forgiveness. Men used to ask forgiveness for having left her for another woman who finally turned up to be a ne'er-do-well. *Because only a mother forgives us in this life, / that's the only truth, / the rest is a lie (La casita de mis viejos).*

The sexed woman (that is to say, any woman besides the mother or sister, a perpetual

virgin in the character's fantasy) always implies the possibility of cheating, in fact, she is the embodiment of deception. This judgement, of a very old lineage since it goes back to the Fathers of the Church themselves (1st and 4th century AD) hides a transparent homosexual attitude: another man is admired (the substitute father), only the woman with no genital activity is loved, and one escapes from the sexed woman as she is seen as an instrument of evil. That's why the good friend advises: *Don't let yourself be persuaded, because she is a woman, and, at birth, / cheating was a feeling for her. / She lies when she cries, she lies when she laughs, / she lies when she kisses and loves (Don't fool yourself, my heart).*

After the indefensible deception, the scene is completed when the tango protagonist accepts that there is no greater happiness than *living with mom again (Victoria)* and that the best thing to say to a woman is —as Celedonio Flores said— *I love you the way I love my mother (Cuando me entres a fallar)*. Everything seems to derive from the firm belief that, *There is only one mother / and even if, one day, I forgot her / she taught me in the end / that to this love / you have to come back (Madre hay una sola), because there is no noblest / or purest affection / for me (Madre)*. After all she is the only affection without deception. That's why Carlos Bahr can say... *For me you are greater than God... / because if the latter is sometimes implacable / with those who make mistakes like me... / you, my mother, because of your kindness and motherhood / are the purest image of forgiveness... (Avergonzado)*, an exaggeration that, for a strict theology constitutes, no doubt, a heresy.

As a way of avoiding an unpleasant, hostile reality where the woman in any of her multifaceted images is always the embodiment of fraud, the character, once he has become disillusioned with the hypnotic feminine charms, is left no alternative but to come back to the protection of the maternal cloister, the warm uterus where apart from avoiding the external aggression, he will be safe from any contamination. Thus, once the protagonist has realized that the woman he loved only needed him

My folks' little house

Quiet neighborhood of my past,
as a sad evening,
I come back to your corner old...
I come back older,
life has changed me...
it left me some silver on my head.

Lyrics by Enrique Cadícamo
Music by Juan Carlos Cobián

Washerwoman in the yard of
a tenement house. 1899.

to pay her a mink coat, admits that the coat in the end, lasted more than your love, because *I'm still paying the coat / and your love is over (Aquel tapado de armiño). And he recognized in another tango: Paying old crazy things / and drowning my sad complaints / I went back to my mother /looking for that profound tenderness / that I had left, / and on seeing me she didn't say a word / about my blunders of the past, / I've only heard /sweet loving words / for her son.*

Once he has come back, the character does not want to hear new siren songs; the best thing to do is to stay home: *I wish that nobody would come to drag me out / from the one who adores me, / who, with a beneficial faith, / strives to comfort me when I feel my old pain. / Temptations to get around her love are useless... / I'm always a boy for her... (Madre hay una sola).* In *Tengo miedo*, Flores repeats: *Today, as you can see, I lead a peaceful life, that's why I simply / beg you not to disturb my sweet peace, / to leave me with my mother, since next to her, I will saintly / build another life for I feel capable of doing so.*

The protagonist of *La casita de mis viejos* repeats the pattern: he comes back defeated after being traveler of pain in an itinerary which led him to alcohol and women *(I blotted out each kiss with a drink).* He tries to justify himself: it was due to a lack of experience: *youthful crazy things, / the lack of some advice,* which also implies a reproach to his parents who were not able to keep him by their side. That's why, on seeing his mother with *her eyes clouded with tears / as if she was asking "why did it take you so long,* he promises, as the rest of the prodigal sons of tango: *Never again shall I go away / and next to you I will feel / the warmth of a great affection...* By contrast, Cadícamo had defined in the first verse: *Women are always those / who kill all hopes. On the mother's lap, shelter and affection;* outside, dangers, defeat, old age. Outside, you suffer, you grow and growth inevitably leads to death. Inside, fantasy allows you to imagine that you are still a boy, as the protagonist of *Madre hay una sola* says.

In view of this way of thinking, it seems only natural that, since his mother lacked a spouse, the tango man —once he has suffered the feminine "deceptions"— should prefer to become a single man. This confirmed bachelor establishes, in fact, a maternal-filial couple appearing time and time again in tango lyrics, but since it is an asexual relationship it implies a great deal of frustration for both parties, which is overcome by a sense of security. The mother senses beforehand a protected old age and the son understands that that responsibility prevents him from having new love affairs. There are two ways of "settling down", of growing: on the first hand, a fully rewarding way, that is to say, by having a family, and, on the other hand, a frustrating way, by remaining with the mother. Anyway, this second alternative keeps him away from the woman's contact and infection, because *You better not talk about them. / All of them, my friend, are worthless... (Tomo y obligo)*. In addition, experience teaches since ancient times that, according to Homero Manzi's maxim, *no trust should be put in women* or, in other words: *It has to be a woman to betray you*, as it is proclaimed by the character in *En la vía*.

That's why around the 1920s, the lyrics Verminio Sevetto wrote for Francisco Pracánico's music were an essential truth and hence the repetition of the subject matter by different artists. The verses showed the strong porteño Oedipus complex: *Mother, the sorrows made me feel low / and I cried without your love, / when I went to pieces at night / because of my deep pain... / Mother, there is nothing nobler or deeper for me than your affection... / The disappointments redeem, / and I came back to my soul's memories... (Madre, recorded by Carlos Gardel in 1922)*.

A poet like Homero Manzi who would produce some of the best literary tango texts, could not escape from this subject matter either; when he was a teenager, he wrote a maternal waltz: In her memory*: Today, my dear mo- ther, / filled with nostalgia for the past, / those sweet moments of joy, / which were forgotten in the name of pleasure, / are coming to me*. This work purely imitates José Betinotti's line when he sang: *My poor dear mother / I've made her suffer so much / what a lot of time, poor thing / I've found her on a corner / crying

deeply hurt /crying deeply hurt (Pobre mi madre querida)*. Verses that contain the oedipal fantasy of being everything for the mother who does not cry because she misses a sexual partner, but because of her son's indiscretions. With an omnipotent feeling, the son takes it for granted that he'd occupy every empty space, tries to block the feeling related to the man's absence and is the only cause of her mother's interest.

While, from time to time, this subject matter reappeared in the verses of some tango artists who were not very popular *(Porque no la tengo más, La vieja vale más)*, this filial concern disappeared coinciding with the argentine industrialization which was consolidated around the 1940s. With the new social laws, the working profile changed as well. From that moment, the man who used to live like a dropout and had to make do with temporary jobs, was included into the factories' payroll and tended to establish his own family. New neighborhoods were born, and the old ones grew. The industrial workers became sedentary persons. In these security conditions, the family units began to develop. On the other hand, those who still lived in social isolation, did not sing tangos anymore: for the most part, they resorted to another kind of music that reminded them of the provincial interior which they had left in search of better economic prospects. The pseudo folk singer, Antonio Tormo, became the undisputed idol for this large sector of people who arrived in the large cities' suburbs, especially in Buenos Aires, during the peronist regime. As the sociological profile changed, its products changed as well, and the "maternal" subject matter soon became a topic of a bygone era.

Esquina Porteña, *tempera on paper by Susana Aguirre. Zurbarán Collection. 1995.*

You must open up, my heart, like a rose, and let the scent of your suburban love affairs fill the air of life. *Gotan*! The music of the people, the slow moan of mouths that cannot groan, but row about their pains to the sound of the little organ. Gotan! The joy that expands and roars with laughter smelling alcohol, and gradually vanishes into the grimace of a cruel smile that branded it for life with a wild and pugnacious grin.

Do not lie a praise with honeyed and mawkish words.

Tell what you know about the sensual, deep, painful and bitter gotan, about this music rich in deep, gloomy, plebeian, pensive emotions; emotions emerging from the tough heart of the infectious outskirts and the luxurious cabaret where unhealthy splendors shine a light into the tormented soul of the chicks who gave themselves to life.

Máximo Sánz
(Last Reason)

Gotán
praise

The Paseo de Julio *and the Central Station. Circa 1890.*

Tango is no longer a simple dance of pleasure breaking itself into spasmodic positions and love provocation's. The song has redeemed it. The song, perhaps a poetic mumbling, has put in the music the aphrodisiac miracle of its simple, honest and sad emotion.

Thus, sometimes the bandoneon's voice becomes hoarse with a cry of pain or shouts of despair and, thus, the suburbs redeem themselves from the sin of their melodic lust, singing to the nasal song of the bando, the melancholy dark hours which are the dark background of their worried and painful life...

Gotan! We have made you to give the milonga a cause of joy and your voice turned hoarse singing the sadness of the *milonguero* life.

You were made to be sensual and you turned out to be sensual among sobs. The electric lights were turned on in order to give you

an ostentatious adornment, and in the same luxurious cabaret, your *mistonga* yearning turned on the lamp of the room that watches over the sad sleep of the dandy that is tossing and turning, unable to sleep, full of jealousy and cowardly impotence because he cannot beat the rotten swine that blew from site.

Later, flighty and giddy, you too, as the chicks from your cradle, went to Paris, looking a *jai* guy, a real *shusheta*.

Gotan! You are the voice, cry, and sob of the people who only laugh when they are drunk. And thus, sad, mad, surly and resentful, as the big city's soul, where the foreign air does arrive, it's true, but only to become impregnated with the nasal melopoeia emerging from the bandoneons.

And now, let me remember the divine moment when tango sounds like an invitation to dance.

Then, the moaning melody takes possession of the rabble's soul and gets into the girls' little heart. Then, emotion firmly holds on to the flesh and bites it without letting go.

The whole being sings on the inside the song of the sad, funereal, ferocious love that wanders through the gloomy city thirsty for pleasure.

The men go up; their heads turn with the intention of falling asleep on the cushion offered by the girl's long hair; she yields to the man's *quebrada* and follows with her body the body that marks the movement.

And down there, the legs intertwine, look for, rub and kiss each other, from the hip to the ankles.

Tango leads. Tango has intoxicated the couples with its strong poison of suffocated pleasure and when the bandos stop singing, his and her eyes keep wandering through the dark world of sensual ecstasy.

Miguel A. Camino

Tango

It was born in the Corrales Viejos,
back in the eighties.
It was the son of a milonga
and a tough guy of the outskirts.
The horn of a streetcar conductor
was its godfather,
and the knife duels
taught him to dance.

    Thus, forming the eight
and the sit-in,
the half-moon,
and the step backwards
he reflected
the charge
and the body clashes
of those who risk their neck
with their knives.

Later, he wore a wide-brimmed hat,
curly hairs, braided trousers,
and patent leather ankle boots.
He went to cheap bars,
restaurants and... inns
and in the *chinas'* bodies
he curled up his virtues.

    Through the *corrida*
and the "fan",
the half short
and the step backwards,
he placed the curves
of his young,
brave man desires,
who gets killed
for the female.

He also wandered through the streets
with a carnation on his ear;
he wore military-like ankle boots.
He took over the tenement house,
he sweet-talked the maids
and thanks to him
everyone learned to whistle.

    And since then
the *malevo* was seen,
sensuality-stricken,
stealing the curves
of the hips,
breasts and legs
of the city chicks.

And the policemen
threw him out of the corner,
he went to Europe,
from where he came back as a gentleman.
He came back with plenty of hair gel,
wearing formal dress
and in the band of streets and *pianolas*
he lost even his curls.

    And today he's a jaife,
sad and skinny guy,
who dances with
a sleepy look;
and his small steps
already look like
those of an old horse
of some *Mateo*
about to quit.

Carlos Cañás: El pensamiento triste
que se baila, *oil painting.*

Ulyses Petit de Murat

Tango

Still
in the open nights of the summer
with somewhat sad breasts and faded
eyes in the shadows. Inside
the rooms shutting
the children's sleep away
the handicapped chairs
the dark desperation of the rags
the hard, darkened mirrors.

Still
with a bitter taste in the mouth
the soul barely awake.
Further away, the blurred streets
the sour cavities
the limp ditches, with no stars
and a sad night dampness of garbage.

The hot vertex of the legs
among a sad night dampness of garbage.
The black mouths were delirious
among a sad night dampness of garbage.

The devoured eyes
the wet hands and the bitter
hips dripping their black, rancorous blood
between blind, corrupted windows
under a forgotten
ash-gray sky, towards which
an insistent, final, hard, fierce
sad night dampness of garbage
goes up.

Jorge Iglesias: Nocturno en la Boca, *oil painting.*

José Gobello

Tomorrow

Do you remember when begging
And crying like a child,
One night you asked me
A little bit of tenderness;
And believing you sincere
All my love I gave to you,
And now without giving you a reason
You have gone away from me.

Music and Lyrics: A. G. Villoldo

To talk about *tanguedad* or *tanguidad* is not correct because the Spanish suffixes —*dad*, —*edad and* —*idad* only appear in abstract nouns derived from adjectives. However, there has to be a way of calling the tango substance, the hipoheimenos mentioned by Aristotle; St. Thomas Aquinos' quidditas, that substance we describe as *compadrón*, sentimental, *porteño*, virile, *malevo*, sleepyhead, and so on. That's why, some people have created the word *tanguedad* or *tanguidad*. We could ask ourselves, therefore, what *tanguedad* is, but let us ask ourselves what is tango, which is the substance of tango.

There are many answers. For some people, tango is the two-four beat, something they often say referring to the four-eight beat; for others, it is an entity you can dance to; for Borges it is a memory of bravery; for some people, it is Gardel's victorious voice emerging from the record player; for others it is bold virility. Some people do not distinguish between different essences and qualities, but between chronologies, and for them Villoldo's affairs and Contursi's tears are the same things, there's no difference between the vivacity of *El Choclo* and the *bolero*-like slowness of *Nostalgias*, but they say tango ends where its own ability to renew itself seems to have disappeared, and thus, some people choose Firpo, others go as far as De Caro, some persist with Salgán, and very few go as far as Piazzolla.

What is, then, the substance of tango, that which underlies the harmonious noise of the orchestras, the singers' racked voices, the dancers' display? Is it sadness, melancholy or nostalgia? No, because tango was already tango when it was cheerful; in fact, it was cheerful, perhaps too cheerful, at birth. Did its substance change when it got sentimental? Nobody, except Borges, would dare to say such a thing. And that's because neither joy nor sadness, neither the rigid time, stylization, syncopation, the illiteracy with a good ear for music, nor virtuosity are the substance of tango. The substance of tango is the ability to express the *porteño*'s, and, by extension, the argentinie's feelings. And thus, when the *porteño*, after bleeding to death in necessary or unnecessary

wars, looked for joy and went on a spree, tango became a reveler... And when the *porteño* —with a lot of *gringo* blood in his veins— merged into the immigrated nostalgia, tango became sentimental, but it was still tango as the *porteño* was still *porteño*. And when the free and obligatory education made him stop bragging, tango followed in the same direction. And when the media started to globalize the people's feelings, tango globalized its melody. And when the *porteño*, partly because of his education and partly due to his mimetic nature, began to feel himself more cultured, tango also threw its naiveté into the attic and became more refined in the styles of Galván, Piazzolla and Stampone. Throughout this process, the porteño, who still was *porteño*, did not lose his substance, and tango did not lose it either.

But the process has not ended. While today's *porteño* is not yesterday's, he is not tomorrow's either. The current tango is not tomorrow's tango either; for some people, the former is the latest Thule. Because if the porteño changes, tango cannot stand motionless without losing its substance.

If you want an eternal tango you need to accept an ever-changing tango, because the substance of tango is neither found in the two-four beat, nor in the four-eight beat, but in change. And the permanent change demands a permanent research, a permanent experimentation. If you want an eternal tango you must accept the fatal fact that you cannot bathe in the same tango twice, and tango must accept the fatal fact that it cannot express the same *porteño* twice. The *porteño*, tango —would say Heraclitus— do not remain still they are always becoming something new.

Attitudes and behaviors which still remain. Tango is always present on each corner.

Manuel Gálvez

Men in loneliness

Ibiza got up violently and joined the group. He looked at everybody with a stomach-ache expression and, with a voice that went hoarse of anger, he exclaimed:

—Here, only tango and football are really in their element. We gave nothing to the world except tango and hair gel. That's, so far, our contribution to human progress.

—Don't speak ill of tango; it's marvelous! protested Maruja.

She had expressed herself with such an enthusiasm that, on realizing it and, above all, on noticing Soltengo's evil look, she blushed.

Maruja had inherited two ways of being sensual. That coming from her *criollo* blood

Art and color for our city.
Two expressions of the Paseo de la Paz, on del Tejar Avenue (today Ricardo Balbín) and Drago St.

and that from her Semitic blood. She had, therefore, her reasons for feeling tango. That's why, she was a little ashamed of herself for revealing them in front of several people, men and women.

She thought she had told a serious secret. Or she remembered a moment of shady pleasure experienced with tango.

—Let's see. Why is it marvelous?–, reprehended her Ibiza, with feverish eyes and planting herself in front of her.

Maruja was totally disconcerted by this almost rude attitude.

—I'll tell you why—, interrupted Claraval.
—Tango is marvelous because there is color,

The perfect integration of ruined walls into visual art.

richness of lines, feeling, harmony, rhythm, suffering in it. It's classic and profound. Almost all of the lyrics are stupid, but its music has a profound and very human meaning. We can expect from the people who have created such a sensitive music as tango, great things in the artistic field. In this country where people and things are expressionless, the expression of tango...

—What does tango express, anyway?—, interrupted Ibiza, almost grumbling.

—Tango is the only real expression of Buenos Aires which is, in turn, an expression and a summary of Argentina. It's all instincts, as us, who have always lived an ins-

tinctive, ill-reasoned, not very intellectual life. Tango, since it belongs to the sensitive and subconscious world, is anti-intellectual, as is the argentine essence; and, since it belongs to the world of feelings and creative instinct, it's against what is mechanic and collective.

You may find in tango many of our essential characteristics. That's why it's the expression of our passivity, our fundamental sadness, our languid sensuality, our laziness, our grief.

—And our loneliness— added Brígida.

—And our separation...— said Dalila, as if she was talking to herself.

Ernesto Sabato

Tango is something serious, my boy

The coolness of the breeze cleared Martin's head. D'Arcángelo was still mumbling things and it took him a while before he could calm down. Then he asked him where he worked. Somewhat embarrassed, Martín answered that he was unemployed. D'Arcángelo looked at him.

—Since when?

—Since a long time.

—Do you have a family?

—No.

—Where do you live?

Martín delayed the answer: he had blushed, but fortunately (he thought) it was dark. D'Arcángelo stared at him.

—In fact... he muttered.

—What?

—Hmm... I had to leave my room...

—Where are you staying now?

Martín, feeling embarrassed, mumbled he slept anywhere. And so as to tone down the fact, he added:

—It isn't so cold yet, anyway.

Tito stopped and examined him under the light of a streetlamp.

—But at least do you have enough to eat?

Martín kept quiet. This made D'Arcángelo blew up:

—Why on earth didn't you say anything! Here I am, talking about tomorrow and you're only pecking at some ingredients. Damn it!

He took him to a cheap restaurant and while they ate, he observed him thougtfully.

When they finished, he adjusted his tie and said:

—Take it easy, boy. Let's go home now. Later, we'll see.

They went into an old coach house that had once belonged to some stately house.

—My old man, you know, was a coachman until ten years ago. Now, because of the rheumatism, he can't move. Besides, nowadays, who will take a coach? My old man is just another victim of the city's progress. Anyway, health is more important than anything else.

It was a mixture of tenement house and stable: you could simultaneously hear shouts, conversations and several radios amid a strong smell of dung. In the old coach houses there were some delivery carts and a small

Constitución Station, c.1895.

truck. You could hear the pounding of the horses' hoofs.

They walked towards the back.

—Here, when I was a little boy, there were three wonderful carriages: the 39, the 42 and the 90. The old man drove the 39. She was a real gem. Not because she belonged to my father, but I guarantee you that she was like a spoiled girl: he painted her, shined her, polished her lanterns. And now, take a look at her.

He pointed to the back, where the coach's carcass lay: she had no lanterns, no wheels, and her cracked canopy was rotten and ripped.

—A few months ago she still went out, poor thing. Nicola, a friend of my father who already died, used to drive her. So much the better, to tell you the truth, because it's better for him to be in the grave than working like that. He did odd jobs; he used to carry parcels.

He caressed the wheel of the old victoria.

—Jesus— he said with a faltering voice, — you should have seen this carriage on the carnival parade in the neighborhood of Barracas. And the old man with the carousel on the coachman's seat. It was a real shock, boy.

Martín asked him if he lived there with the whole family.

—What family are you talking about, boy? We're just my old man and I. My mother died three years ago. My brother Américo is in Mendoza, he works as a house painter, like me. Another one, Bachicha, is married in Mataderos. My brother Argentino, whom we called Tino, was an anarchist and he got killed in Avellaneda, in 1930. A brother who was called Chiquín, died of tuberculosis.

He laughed.

—You know that some of us have weak lungs. I believe it's has to do with a the lead in the paint. My sister Mafalda got married as well and lives in Azul. Another younger brother, Andrés, is a little crazy and we don't even know where he is; I think he's in Bahía Blanca. And then, there's Norma. There's no point talking about her. She's one of these girls who could easily go the whole life going through radio or cinema magazines. She wanted to be an artist. So we were left on our own, my old man and I. That's life, boy: you work, you have children and, in the end, you're only left on your own, like the old man. Thank goodness I'm half crazy and, in addition, no woman notices me, otherwise, who knows, perhaps I would have had to leave too, and the old man would have ended his days, alone, in the gutter.

They went into the room. There were two beds: one of them belonged to his crazy brother who was wandering through Bahía Blanca. So, for the time being, Martín could sleep there. But before that, he showed him his treasures: a dedicated photograph of Américo Tesorieri, nailed to the wall, with an argentine emblem under it: *"To my friend Humberto J. D'Arcángelo"*. Tito stood there staring at it in rapture. Then, he commented:

—The Great Américo.

You could also find on the walls other photos and *El Gráfico* magazine clippings and, on top of everything, a great flag of Boca football team spread lengthwise.

On a crate, he had an old clockwork phonograph with a loud speaker.

—Does it work?— asked Martín.

D'Arcángelo stared at him, with a surprised expression, and almost scolded him:

—Most of today's new record players do not work as well as this one.

He approached the large, dusty loud speaker and cleaned it.

—I would never change it for one of those, not even if they paid me. You know, these things are too complicated. These ones were more natural, and you could listen to the voice as it was.

He put on *Alma en pena* and wound up the old device: Gardel's voice was heard through the loudspeaker, hardly emerging from a tangled web of noises. Tito, his head next to the loudspeaker, shaking it with excitement, muttered: *Great, boy, great!* They remained silent. When the music stopped, Martín saw there were tears in D'Arcángelo's eyes.

—Damn it!—he said, laughing falsely. –All of those who came later were nothing but shit.

He slipped the record into a very old cover, carefully placed it on a pile, while he asked:

—Do you like tango, boy?

—Yes, of course— answered Martín, with caution.

—That's good. Because now, I'm going to be quite honest with you, the new generation knows nothing about tango. Pure fox-trots and that mixture of boleros, rumbas, and all those stupid things. Tango is something serious, something deep. It speaks you to your soul. It makes you think.

He sat on the bed, pondering for some minutes.

—But— he said, "everything is over. Sometimes I think, boy, that everything is over for this country; all the good things are over and won't come back, as the tango says. Tango, football, carnival, everything. I really don't know. And when one of those clowns wants to make a new tango, it's out of the question! Tango must be tango and nothing else. And that's over, boy, that's for sure. It's something that breaks your heart, but it's a truth glaringly obvious.

Then, he added, because he always wanted to be fair:

—Well, perhaps it's an important music, I don't know. Perhaps Piazzolla and those guys today are making something important, serious music, as Strauss' waltzes. I don't deny it. I'm just saying that that's not tango, I guarantee you that, boy.

Later, he told him that his father was not feeling well with his rheumatism, but, above all, he was terribly upset with Bachicha.

—You know— he bitterly explained. — One day he told him he'd sell the 40 and with the pesos he had saved he'd buy a taxi. Imagine how angry the old man was. He got upset, he insulted him, begged, but it was all in vain, because Bachicha is as hard as nails. I swear to God, if, at that moment, I had had a brick I would have thrown it at him. All in vain. He bought the taxi, and to make matters worse, he brought it here. The old man was in bed for more than a month. When he got up, he was not the same person any more.

Then he added:

—Not only did he get his own way, but, to make matters worse, he told him that the coaches were finished, father, he said, you have to resign to the truth, he said, whatever made you think anybody could live with that stuff, he said, don't you realize, father, that we must fit in with progress, he said, don't you understand that the world is moving forward and you insist on maintaining that old wreck, for no reason, because you damn well want to, he said, don't you realize that people want speed, efficiency, he said, that the world must move faster and faster, he said. And each of these words were like a knife.

They went to bed.

Samuel Eichelbaum

The 1900 guapo

A tango is played on a barrel organ. Gualberto goes to the corner and calls the organ-grinder. The tango stops abruptly.

GUALBERTO: —I have a few coins dancing in my pockets.

TESTA: —It looks as if you are going to need the fire brigade from La Boca.

BATARAZ: —That's true, man. You are showing more joy inside than a party.

From the corner, an old man appears dragging his music machine.

GUALBERTO *(to the organ-grinder)*: —Come on, old man. Crank that thing with all your strength.

The old man plays his barrel organ from which a great tango emerges. The boys and men get a partner among themselves and dance in a ritual way.

BATARAZ *(to his partner)*: —Don't hurry! Tango is danced with the whole life ahead of you. You have to listen to the beat than to your own mother.

TESTA *(to his partner)*: —I cant' dance with you! You come on top of me and I cant' move.

YIYO: —Take a look at me and learn how to dance this. To think that there are people who say that nobody can be a born dancer. Nobody taught me anything and...look: I'm the master of tango!—

GUALBERTO: —Hey, you, stuck-up, shut up! Stop dancing. What a guy! Don't you know yet that you have to dance tango listening to it as if your were listening to an emergency whistle?

A long pause, during which one can only hear the music and sense the dancers' total devotion to the dance.

GUALBERTO *(The music ends)*: —Another one.

BATARAZ: —Yes, but don't you hurry, my friend. Can't you see that my buddy here is giving me trouble?

GUALBERTO: —Your buddy?

BATARAZ: —Yes, man. The one I have inside. Isn't it mine? *(Another tango is played in the barrel organ)*.

GUALBERTO *(to Yiyo)*: —Come, let's dance it together.

A girl comes out from one of the houses and heads toward the corner.

GUALBERTO *(when the girl goes right past them)*: —Because of you, women, I have to dance with this fool. Do you want to join me, brunette?

GIRL: —I'm sorry. *(With an open smile)*. —I've a partner for all the party.

GUALBERTO: —So young and already engaged?

GIRL: —That's right!

The girl went on her way. She turns right and disappears. Gualberto and Yiyo start to dance. Other couples do the same.

Lino Palacio: El organillero, *tempera.*

LOS DESTINOS HUMILDES — EL ORGANILLERO

Adolfo Bioy Casares

The dream of the heroes

Later, they had *mate*, Gauna sitting in a chair and the doctor in the Vienna armchair. They almost did not talk. If someone would have seen them from the outside, he would have thought: father and son. Gauna felt that way too.

In the annexed room, Antúnez attacked, for the third time, *La copa del olvido*.

Valerga remarked:

—We must make that noisy guy stop. But first, I want to show you something.

I saw him rummaging about his closet for a while. He came back with a small bronze spade, and declared:

—With this spade, doctor Saponaro put the mortar on the cornerstone of the chapel around the corner.

Gauna piously took it and studied it, marveled at the object. Before putting it away, Valerga, gave it a quick rub to brought out the shine in those bronze parts which were touched by the boy's inexperienced and moist fingers. Valerga took out something more from that inexhaustible closet: a guitar. When his young friend obsequiously tried to examine it, Valerga took him aside and said:

—Let's go to the study.

Antúnez was singing, perhaps less lively than other times, *Mi noche triste*. Brandishing the guitar triumphantly, the doctor asked with a thunderous and dull voice:

—Tell me something, who in their right mind would sing just like that, without any accompaniment if there is a guitar in the house?

Everybody, including Antúnez, sincerely laughed at this funny remark, maybe encouraged by the intuition that tension had been defused. Besides, all you had to do was look at Valerga to notice he was in a good mood. The young men, already free of fears, cried their laugh.

—Now, you're going to see— announced the doctor, while he moved Antúnez away and sat, —what this old man can do with the guitar.

Smiling, with no rush, he started to tune it. From time to time, his skillful and nervous strumming, showed an incipient melody. Then, with a very gentle voice, he sang softly:

On the path,
the unhappy mother,
preparing mate,
in the afternoons.
He stopped singing to point out:

—No tangos, boys. Leave it for the malevos and madam violinists.—Then he added with a hoarse voice— Or the vegetable slaughtermen.

With a beatific smile, loving hands, slowly, as if time did not exist, he started to tune the guitar again. He amused himself singing those songs, which did not bore him, until midnight. There was a general feeling of cordiality, of a friendly and sensitive happiness. Before asking them to leave, the doctor ordered Pegoraro to bring some beer and glasses from the kitchen. They drank a toast to everybody's happiness.

The immigrants brought their loneliness and music.
Tango was fueled by their feelings.

Two-four beat

Dances and "compadritos"

Homero Manzi

Discepolín

On the frozen marble, crumbs of croissants
and an absurd woman eating in a corner...
Your muse is bleeding and she's having breakfast...
dawn doesn't forgive and is heartless.
In the end, who's to blame for the grotesque life
and the soul stained with carmine blood?
We'd better go out before dawn,
before we cry, old Discepolín!

I'm aware of your long boredom
and I understand how hard it is to be happy,
and to the sound of each tango I feel your presence
with your huge talent and your nose;
with your bitter and hidden tears,
with your pale, clownish mask,
and with that saddened smile
that flourishes in verse and song.

People move closer to you with a pile of sorrow
and you caress them almost shaking...
Other people's scars hurt you as if they were yours:
that guy was not lucky and this girl had no love.
The dance floor began to fill to the noise of the orchestra...
they embrace each other under the spotlight as sawdust dolls...
Can't you see they're dancing? Can't you see they're
    partying?
Let's go, everything hurts, old Discepolín...

*Pages 90-91: Carnival
and tango in a dance at
the Victoria Theater. 1901.*

Enrique Santos Discépolo

Why and how I write tangos

I write tangos because I find its rhythm attractive. I feel in it an intensity only sensed in very few other things. Its synthesis is a challenge which rouses me and which I accept with pleasure... To say so many things in such a short time. What a difficult and beautiful thing!

To write a tango I mentally distribute the central events. I divide the conflict in different parts and, taking into account the state (I mean, the psychological state), the state of mind, I try to talk about it with music. I follow the character in his grief, his joy and his rage. I have never thought about the other "State", with a capital letter. If I had done that, I would have avoided the suspension of my songs on the radio. Sometimes, on following my characters through their joy and their rage, I dislocate my music, something that surprises and bothers many musicians. They say I sacrifice the melody line to the lyrics, and that's not true. I deliberately break the musical image because I feel impelled to do so. I want the music to say what the lyrics will later explain even further. Through the very few words of the lyrics of a tango, a whole story lives, jumps, quiets down, cries, laughs, talks, curses or gets upset. How could it be possible for the music to be independent from that?

A tango is a free expression. Its structure and its constructive technique purely depends on the subject matter which moves it to sing, thus bringing it to life. The great musicians will never be able to create an expressive tango. Their mathematical, technical characteristic, which is per se rejected by tango, prevent them from doing so.

I use slang for the very simple reason that it allows me a better description. There are states of mind or kind of places for which the academic words cannot be used and are unsuitable. I don't understand why "stealing" is more suitable than "nicking". Is it habit? Who cares...? The thing is that there are nasty words and pretty words...

Both the Academy and slang have countless words I don't like. From both of them I use those I like for their categorical, pictorial or sweet taste. Some of them are large, curved, schmaltzy, bereaved. And you can find

Enrique Santos Discépolo, in his radio program
Mordisquito. *Circa 1950.*

them in every language. And if my country, which is cosmopolitan and Babylonian, on handling them every day, understands them and I need them, I lasso them full of joy. Our slang shows some marvelous phonetic characteristics. They want to kill it. They make me laugh. Those who believe languages have been created by wise men are really funny. If people's need is capable of creating a genius, how could anybody stop them from creating a particular word? And slang, almost in its entirety, stands out precisely for that. Its words are always more graphic than those it replaces, more powerful and more ours. In *Soy un arlequín* I did not use it because I did not need it...

My songs emerge as follows: I'm strolling along Corrientes and a tango appears in my ear. First, I think of the lyrics, that is to say, the subject matter. I give the matter a lot of thought. And suddenly, when I am sitting at a café's table, reading at home or walking along the streets, the music matching that state of mind, that tango situation, begins to sound in my ears. And that's when tragedy emerges because of my lack of knowledge. I hardly play a few notes on the piano. I have learnt to play violin only for a year and a half, and I never could play it well. And of course I can't write music. As soon as the tango begins to whistle in my ear, I run in search of a friend so that he can write it for me. Many times, I can't find one right away. And that's when I begin to get desperate because I don't want these notes, which appeared to me out of the blue —because it's like that: they just appear— to be lost. Then, I begin to sing them. And I keep singing them aloud. Even if I'm walking down the street and everybody looks at me as if I were crazy. Even if I am in a café, and everybody turns around to me. At that moment, nothing matters. The only thing I am interested in is not to allow the tango to slip away. I only try to keep singing it until somebody comes to tie it to paper. But the street is always the origin of tango. That's why, I walk through the city trying to enter its soul, imagining in my sensitivity what this man or this girl who are going past would like to hear, what they would sing in a happy or painful moment in their lives...

Many tangos have been written in moments of despair. The song has emerged from the authors as a reaction, as a liberation, when faced with a hard situation. Once this situation has disappeared, tangos which were only the expression of pain, sadness or rage, come to an end. Without even thinking of it, I probably wrote when I felt the need for them. That same need is also felt by others and that's when tango becomes successful. The character of my tangos is Buenos Aires, the city. Some sensitivity and a bit of observation have provided the subject matter for all of my lyrics.

I wrote my first tango during hard times. I lived with Armando in an apartment and he had already planned the play *Stéfano*. We just had to start working but, despite the absolute urge to carry on with the work in the hope of getting around a hard situation, I was the one who failed... When it was time to start writing, I used to disappear in an attic with my guitar... I used there the strangest method. I composed a line, tried to play it on the guitar and then, watching the position of the fingers, I used to write it with two numbers, one for the guitar fret and the other for the number of chords. And that was enough. By means of this kind of notes, which I still use, I used to learn the piece of music by heart; played by me, it could then be transcribed on the pentagramby any friend of mine who could write music...

As for the topics, I did not write with the intention of enhancing tango, but of giving it a human, real meaning...

Enrique Santos Discépolo

Cambalache

I already know
that the world has been and will be a load of rubbish;
in five hundred and six
and in the year 2000 as well;
that there had always been thieves,
Machiavellis and swindlers,
happy and bitter,
genuine and fake people,
nobody denies that
the twentieth century is a display
of insolent evilness any more;
we live wallowing in a mess
and everybody in the same mud.

So now it seems that
being honest or a traitor,
ignorant, wise, thief,
pretensious, swindler,
is just the same thing.
Everything is the same; nothing is better;
a dumb or a great professor, it makes no difference.
There are neither failures nor scales;
those who have no morals have equaled us.
If there's one who lives as an impostor
and another steals out of ambition,
it makes no difference whether he's a priest,
a mattress maker, king of the *bastos* suit,
a cheeky devil or a stowaway.

What a lack of respect,
what an outrage against reason;
anybody is a gentleman,
anybody is a thief.
Stavisky is mixed up with
Don Bosco and the Mignon,
Don Chicho and Napoleon,
Carnera and San Martín.
As in the disrespectful shop window
of the *cambalaches* (thrift stores)
life has been mixed up,
and wounded by a saber with no rivets
you can see the Bible crying next to a boiler.

Twentieth century, cambalache,
and feverish;
he who doesn't ask, doesn't get,
and he who doesn't steal is a jerk.
Come on, anything goes,
but in hell, we are going to meet anyway.
Stop thinking, step aside,
nobody cares if you were born honest.
There's no difference between a man who works
night and day like as an ox,
with a man who lives on the others,
than the one who kills and the one who heals
or is an outlaw.

Jacinto Chiclana, *painting by Rodolfo Ramos*
(Zurbarán Collection).

Enrique Santos Discépolo

*Page 97: From the roof of the Casa Rosada,
aiming in vain at hard times.
It's the 1930 coup.*

Yira... Yira...

When luck, which is a woman
failing you time and again,
deserts you;
when you are down to your last penny,
when you've lost your bearings, desperate;
when you neither have faith
nor yesterday's *mate* leaves
drying under the sun;
when you wear out your shoes
looking for enough money
to eat, only then
you feel
the indifference of the world,
that is deaf and mute.

You'll see that everything is a lie,
you'll see that nothing is love,
that the world couldn't care less...
Yira... Yira...

Even though your life breaks,
even though a pain bites you,
don't ever wait help,
a hand or a favor.

When the batteries of every
door bell you have rung
looking for a fraternal chest
to die
have gone flat;
when you've been thrown away
after working so hard
the same as I have;
when you realize that next to you
they are trying on the clothes
that you'll leave behind,
you will remember this fool
who one day, tired,
started to bark.

*Eviction from a tenement
house. 1931.*

Enrique Cadícamo

Anchored in Paris

Ditched in the life of a wandering bohemian
I am, Buenos Aires, anchored in Paris.
On the wrong side of life, covered with constraints,
I remember you from this distant country.
I contemplate the snow falling softly
from my window that opens onto the boulevard;
the reddish lights with a dying shade
are like pupils with a strange look.

Distant Buenos Aires, you must be so beautiful!
You saw me setting sail almost ten years ago...

Here, in this Montmartre, sentimental *faubourg*,
I feel the memory plunging its dagger into my body.

Your Corrientes street must have changed a lot!
Suipacha, Esmeralda, even your suburb!...
Someone has told me you're flourishing
and that there's a set of streets running diagonally...
You don't know how much I want to see you!
I am stuck here, with no money and no faith...
Who knows? Death may catch me one night
and, bye-bye Buenos Aires, I won't see you again!

The Graf Zeppelin *blimp crosses the sky of
Buenos Aires. 1934.*

Mural painting, tribute to Homero Manzi on Centenera Ave. and Tabaré St., with allegories about Malena, Che bandoneón, *and* El último organito.

Hipólito Jesús Paz

Before and after the "Maestro"

The person who took me out, I believe it was in 1926, to the Select Lavalle theater to listen to Julio de Caro's orchestra, was a character who filled my childhood. It was my aunt, my mother's sister, called Julia but whom, God knows why, we called "Tata", the one who took me across the threshold of tango. Her great refinement and her love for every expression of beauty, her youthful curiosity which she kept right up to her death, her joy *de vivre* and class, which allowed her to disregard the conventions when they became something ridiculous and inhuman, defined her soul.

In short, she was "someone", would have said Flaubert. And to top it all, she felt love for tango. As soon as I was five years old she took me out to the Empire theater that day, which became for me a special date, located on the corner of Maipú street and Corrientes, to listen to the Gardel-Razano duo.

But this first contact with De Caro at the Select Lavalle theater was ephemeral. Only two years later —when I was still a boy— was I able to enjoy regularly the music of this ensemble which is thought to divide the history of tango, from the orchestral point of view, into two periods: before and after its appearance.

What I am about to narrate took place at the beginning of 1928, at the end of Dr. Alvear's Administration, who was a great ruler and, incidentally, one of Julio De Caro's many admirers as well. I must admit that, on making an inventory of this last half century, I remember yesterday's world and I'm filled with melancholy.

Back then, the Maestro left the downtown of the city in order to make his debut at one of the more elegant theaters in the northern area of town: the Petit Splendid. It was located on Libertad street, facing the square, a few meters from the *Paris Café*, and was what would be called today an exclusive place. My parents' home was only one block from the theater — at Cerrito street, between Paraguay Street and Córdoba— and, together with my younger sisters and the sitter who accompanied them, we inexorably went on thursdays and sundays to devour the program from beginning to end. On sundays, the program started at 2 p.m. and ended at 8.30 p.m., and we used to leave behind the echoes of our father's protests who

Page 101: Julio De Caro next to Julio Jorge Nelson and Ben Molar, at the Fulgor Club, in Villa Crespo. 1978.

predicted we would go blind. With the tickets in our hands and the best seats thanks to the ticket-seller's favoritism, a man whose name I won't forget, "Chaparra", we installed ourselves at the theater's doors at 1.45 p.m., waiting for the ushers who were rather short twin brothers whom we had nicknamed "the dwarfs", and who used to show up with a Valentino hairstyle, wearing stunning uniforms.

And De Caro went there and performed a miracle: he imposed tango. Of course he played in the evening performances. The round of applause turned many times into an ovation and the "encores" were frequent.

Years later, on chatting with my old, dear and admired friend Julio, he told me that season had been one of the greatest satisfactions of his life.

With my younger sister, with whom we shared a passion for tango, we will never forget those evenings at the Petit Splendid. How could we possibly erase from our minds the memory of the interpretations of *El Monito, Tierra negra, Lorenzo, Sobre el pucho, La última cita* and so many other tangos...?

At that time, if I remember right, the orchestra was made up of the following musicians: Pedro Laurenz and Armando Blasco, "the little blind", on bandoneon; Francisco De Caro on piano; Vicente Sciarreta, looking really good, on double bass, and Emilio and Julio De Caro, on violin. I think the singer was Pedro Lauga.

Each of those names is a chapter in the history of tango in itself. Julio De Caro managed to offer with his orchestra an unprecedented and lasting voice in the universe of our music.

The Maestro has been highly praised as a virtuoso, composer or conductor. But all that is not much compared to what he really is and represents.

My dear Julio: in short, this is what I wanted to tell you. Since the first time I listened to your orchestra, you dazzled me. Today, at this stage, your memory and that of those distant days at the Petit Splendid, are as a pleasant light that knock the rough edges off life. Thank you.

Café de los Angelitos...

Bar of Gabino and Cazón...
I brought you happiness with my shouts
in the days of Carlitos
on Rivadavia Street and Rincón...

Lyrics by José Razzano
Music by Cátulo Castillo

Homero Manzi

Che, bandoneón

The magic of your voice, che bandoneon,
takes pity on the others' pain
and on squeezing your sleepy bellows
it comes closer to the most ailing heart.
Estercita and Mimí, as Ninón,
leaving behind their percale fate,
wore at the end
rayon shrouds
to the funereal echo of your song.

Bandoneon,
today it's *fandango* night
and I want to confess you the truth,
one glass, one pain, one tango after the other,
excited by insanity
alcohol and bitterness.
Bandoneon,
what's the point of mentioning her so much?
Can't you see my heart wants to forget her,
and she comes back, night after night, as a weeping
in the notes of your song,
che, bandoneon.

Your song is the love that didn't happen
and the sky we once dreamed about
ant the fraternal friend who fell down
fighting in the middle of the storm of a love affair...
And sometimes, for no reason at all,
we feel like bursting into tears
and there's the swig of liquor
which forces us to remember
that the soul is offside, che, bandoneón.

Aníbal Troilo, *oil painting by Bourse Herrera.*

Cátulo Castillo

The last drunkenness

Bandoneon, your hoarse, malevo curse
hurts my heart;
your tear of rum
takes me
to the deep depths
where mud rises up.
I know, don't tell me,
you're right,
life is an absurd wound
and everything, everything is so ephemeral
that my confession is only the result
of drunkenness, that's all.

Tell me about your hardship,
about your failure,
can't you see the pain that's hurting me?
And simply tell me
about that absent love
behind a piece of oblivion.
I know that weeping
my wine speech hurts you,
I know you're feeling a deep pain
but it's the old love
that shivers, bandoneon,
trying to find in a stunning liquor
a final drunkenness
that will end the show
and lower the curtain for my heart.

Your slow telling-off drips
some memories and heartaches;
your liquor makes me dizzy
and rushes my heart beat
on spilling the final drunkenness.
Close the large window for me
as the sun is burning
its slow snail of sleep
can't you see I come from a country
plunged into oblivion, always gray,
of alcohol?

Bandoneonista, *oil painting
by Juan Carlos Castagnino.*

Ricardo Güiraldes

Tango

Tango severe and sad.
Threatening tango.
Tango in which every note drops heavily, as if out of spite, under a
    hand which seems destined
to grab a knife handle.
Tragic tango, which melody plays with a fight topic.
Slow rhythm, complicated harmony of hostile counterpoints.
A dance in which the spirits clouded by alcohol are caught up in a virile whirl.
Creator of mute silhouettes gliding under the hypnotic
    action of a bloody dream.
Tilted wide-brimmed hats on rude grimaces.
Demanding love of a tyrant who is jealous of its dominant will.
Females who have given over to submissiveness as obedient beasts.
A complicated laugh of rape.
Brothel's breath. An environment reeking of rude *chinas* and
    sweaty males.
Premonition of a sudden outburst of shouts and threats,
    which will end with a dull groan, a steaming gush
    of blood, as the last, useless protest.
Red spot that coagulates into black.
Fatal tango, arrogant and coarse.
Notes lazily dragged, on a twangy keyboard.
Tango, honest and sad.
Threatening tango.
A dance of love and death.

Celedonio Flores

Corrientes and Esmeralda

Guapos were calmed down next to
        your corner curves
when a fop punched them
and the tough gangs gave you luster
back in... 1902...

Porteño corner, your despicable people
mixes with *gin fitz* eau-de-vie,
pase inglés and *monte*, baccarat and sports
        lottery,
grappa drunkards and drug addict prostitutes.

The Odeón produces the *Real Academia*,
the old Pigall resounds with tangos,
and the bereaved anemia bets all it has
waiting for its streetcar to its suburb.

From Esmeralda northwards, in the direction of
Retiro
some beautiful French chicks show up
in search of a trip with anyone who comes along
avoiding the cop's look.

On your corner, one day, Milonguita, that
beautiful *criolla* chick who was sung by Linning,
carrying a plebeian bundle for the man,
perhaps found tragedy.

Carlos de la Púa describes you in his poems
and the poor Contursi was your faithful friend...
At your loutish corner any old bag
dreams about Gardel's elegance.

Porteño corner, this milonguero
offers you his deepest and most cordial affection.
When you are even with life
I promise you the most despicable and revealing
verse
to create the tango that will make you immortal.

*A typical tango trio: Luis Bussolini, José Chiquetto
and José Aducci.*

Page 105: Tango characters, *ink by Faruk.*

PERSONAJES DE TANGO

MADAME IVONNE   EL CIRUJA   MARIA   EL PENADO 14

ALBERTO ARENAS   LA MOROCHA   HARAGAN   LA MUCHACHA DEL CIRCO

LA RUBIA MIREYA   GARUFA   ESTHERCITA   SHUSHETA

GIUSEPPE EL ZAPATERO   CALLEJERA   PATADURA   LECHUZA

MALENA   EL ENCOPAO   PIPISTRELA   EL LOCO DE LA BALADA

Enrique Cadícamo

The La Cavour dance hall (1907)

La Cavour was a dance hall of ill-tempered people,
which was located at Coronel Salvadores street
between Patricios street and, I believe, Hernandarias street.
A neighborhood of *cuarteadores* and tough guys.

On Saturday night, there was a show and dance.
There, the *filodramático* performed *Justicia Criolla*.
The Centro Parlatutti, moved the audience
and the drama made it cry like the onions.

Emilio Lola was the stage director
of that scene which was praised by everybody.
Then, the actors wore, in the manner of
Pablo Podestá, impressive long hair.

After the show, the chairs were removed
and the dance was already a fact, with Garrote's Orchestra.
This bandoneonist did wonders
and many people of his time danced to his rhythm.

And when the couples went to the dance floor
there was always some trouble related to a dance step.
And while they went round they kept a close eye on each other
and the provocative remarks were the favorite sport.

There was that man who took two ladies as "wild cards"
because he was able to take a "sister-in-law".
And that pimp and two chicks
were able to face any kind of situation.

Sonidos de Buenos Aires, *ink by Graciela Shalev.*

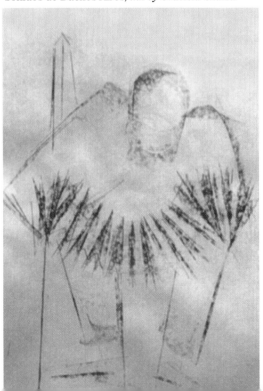

And then, when a *compadrito*
asked one of the girls to dance, he would answer with a lot of nerve:
"She dances with me..." "And the other, young man?"
"She also dances with me... I bring her as a fresh dancer."

If someone recognized in one of them
a friend's wife, it was too much.
After the question, the quarrel
and almost immediately, a brawl that made the walls shake.

They went out into the patio, a sort of scaffold
and once there, they avenged the insult of the cheated friend.
The doors of the lobby were closed from inside
and a disemboweled man remained on the floor.

On other occasions, a tough guy would show up
with his wife whom someone had proposed to run away with.
Later, that man was taken as a guest
and the woman was told to walk in front of him.

And if he didn't ask her to dance, he was forced to
and the husband himself would say:
"Dance with my wife..." And if he refused,
then, they went out into the patio to have a fight.

There was a famous black man nicknamed Chicote,
who danced the waltz to the left.
He danced an hour and twenty minutes and the dancer P.B.T.
still remembers this success.

"Stamina", "Rhythm", "Elegance" and "Gracefulness",
were the conditions imposed on everybody.
The old Buenos Aires certainly polished a lot of floors
on dancing these waltzes which were translated by the bandoneon!

The "Ñato" of Barracas, a cart driver of the old times,
won a great contest, but lost his life.
A fanatic loser, in front of the police officers,
saw him off with shots, when he was coming out of the place.

That's why, during the dance nights one could hear
the coming and going of the black cart of the Argerich
Hospital... And a real mess of tables,
shouts and indecency exploded.

La Cavour was a dance hall of extraordinary fame
which was located on the Coronel Salvadores street,
only frequented by ill-tempered people,
with agile fingers, always ready to pull the trigger.

At a poor old man's pace
the twilight little organ
began to fill the suburb with notes
and a concert of broken glass...

Lyrics by José Gonzáles Castillo
Music by Cátulo Castillo.

The Julio De Caro Sextet in 1925. Julio, Francisco and Emilio
De Caro, Pedro Maffia, Pedro Laurenz and Enrique Krauss.

Horacio Ferrer

Ballad to my death

I shall die in Buenos Aires. It will happen at dawn.
I shall gently put away the things of life:
my little poem of farewell and bullets,
my tobacco, my tango, my handful of spleen.

I shall wrap the whole dawn around my shoulders;
my penultimate whisky will not be drunk.
My death, in love, will *tanguilly* come,
I'll be dead, at six sharp.

Today, that God stops dreaming about me,
I'll head for oblivion through Santa Fe,
I know you're already there, at our corner
all sadness from head to toe!
Hold me tight, as I hear death
inside me, old death,
attacking what I loved...
My dear soul... We're going...
The day is coming... Don't cry!

I shall die in Buenos Aires. It will happen at dawn.
Those who know how to do it die at that moment;
the perfumed bad mood of that verse that I never could
        tell you
will waft along my silence.

I'll walk so many blocks... and there in Plaza Francia,
as shadows escaping from a tired ballet,
my memories, repeating your name down a white
        street,
will go away on tiptoes.

I shall die in Buenos Aires. It will happen at dawn.
I shall gently put away the things of life;
my little poem of farewell and bullets,
my tobacco, my tango, my handful of spleen.

I shall wrap the whole dawn around my shoulders;
my penultimate whisky will not be drunk.
My death, in love, will *tanguilly* come,
I'll be dead at six sharp...

At six sharp.
At six sharp.
At six sharp!

The city and its lights.

Horacio Ferrer

The last grela

A long time ago, they were the romantic proletarians of love. The night found for them names of an insulting seduction: paicas, locas, milongas, percantas, or grelas.

They were often seen at dawn having hot chocolate and churros for breakfast at the "Vesubio" café, on Corrientes street: they finished work at the "Chantecler", the "Marabú" and the "Tibidabo" at that time.

With a fit of madness of Madame Bovary from southern Barracas, they put everything they had on tangos. One of them fell in love with that bandoneonist, and for love, she won; others, were totally defeated: they ended up working in the cloakroom of these same cabarets. Perhaps they left together, one day, as if they were a small and extinct race with rings under the eyes.

This tango tells the story of the last grela. She discovers her final ghostly passage down the streets, at dawn, in a spectral Buenos Aires, and she tells it as follows:

From the bottom of things and wrapped in a stole
of coldness, with the gesture of who has died a lot,
the last, fatal, suburban and lonely *grela* will come,
clicking in the darkness of the smokes.

With wine and bread of the very sweet tango Arolas
stopped playing next to the tired mud of her
      forehead,
the bandoneons and guitars will say their suburban
         mass
playing in the quiet, so mysteriously!

They will say good-bye to her boredom, her cough,
      her melodrama,
the pale, blond-haired women from a short story by
        Tuñón;
and behind the dreamless doorways, the madams
with their tragic long hair will give her the extreme
      unction.

And a dull hoarseness of spleen and nonsense,
like a tango in her soul, will burn her voice.
And, speechless and knelt down, she will sell herself
      without feeling to,
lifeless, for two *pesos* to God's kindness.

Francisco García Jiménez

From the suburbs to the center

Horacio Ferrer: La yumba, tempera. *A tribute to "maestro" Pugliese and to his own rhythm.*

On the corner of Suárez street and Necochea street, the southern *trattorias* had come back with their appetizing *maccheroni* and harmonious *mandulinata* and through the doors of the cafés, the tango instruments had started their exodus, together with those bright waitresses who used to accompany their chords tapping the trays with their knuckles...

The Café Royal Trio splits up. Samuel Castriota goes away, with his pianist and guitarist fingers. Vicente Loduca and his melodious bandoneon went his own way. "Pirincho" Canaro teamed up with bandoneonist Vicente Greco to share their musical passion. Canaro himself told the special circumstances in which this extraordinary performer, a 14 year old precocious musician who excelled himself in flute, guitar and piano, finally chose the bandoneon. Some young men who were serenading, got to the tenement house, on Sarandí street, where Greco lived. Another tenant, a police sergeant who was disturbed in the night, got up angry blowing emergency whistles. The *philharmonics* fled and the bandoneon player gave Greco his instrument so that he could put it away. Since he took some time to get it back, Vicente got interested in playing this instrument and, thanks to his good ear and a miraculous intuition, he later became one of the most outstanding bandoneon virtuosos.

As I said before, Canaro teams up with Greco and, accompanied by Aragón on piano and Pecci on flute, they played at *El Estribo café*, at 763/67 Entre Ríos Street. The audience overflows the place into the sidewalk and the street. The local precinct was forced to send some police officers every night with the purpose of keeping order and a check on the crowd.

The La Argentina Dance Hall

Attracted by the success of the Greco's quartet, Santillán, *El Pardo*, and Aín, "El Vasco", who were dancers, went to the café and looked for the musicians in order to invite them to play in the dancing parties they used to organize at *La Argentina* dance hall, located at 361 Rodríguez Peña Street. *La Argentina*

dance hall successfully competed at the time with other mutual benefit societies founded by a number of italian and spanish honest subjects: "Patria e Lavoro", on Chile street; "Colonia Italiana", on Paraná street; "Unione e Benevolenza", on Cangallo street (today Pte. J. D. Perón); "Orfeón Español", on Piedras street; "Centro de Almaceneros", on Lorca street (today, Presidente Luis Sáenz Peña street), etc. These places were rented to the rather heterogeneous "middle class" of tango a number of nights during the week and on Sunday evening, because the Saturdays were devoted to their own community parties. *La Argentina's* success was due to the fact that it opened its doors to "party", especially those Saturday nights, and was obviously packed. Tango prevailed there freely. The place was halfway between the distant *"La Tucumana"* dance hall, frequented by the lower class, which was lit by kerosene lamps near the Maldonado stream, and "madame" Jeanne's cute house which was located on Maipú street, to the north, with Louis XV furniture and silk drapes.

The stronger sex at *"La Argentina"* wore square long hair, showed hunched shoulders and was not particularly good-looking. The weaker sex (weaker?, "up to a point"...) wore tight-fitting clothes with loud colors... and perfumed itself with *Agua Florida*. At the buffet, gin and anisette were served by the gallon. At the hall, when the struggle to impose *"ochos"* and *"medias lunas"* exceeded every possibility, the most skillful dancer won the laurels writing his name on the floor, with an intangible stroke.

Dance at "La Argentina" hall, the night of its centenary.

The Characters of Buenos Aires *in the neighborhood of La Recoleta.*

Fernán Silva Valdés

Stanzas to the tango of the guardia vieja

Gentlemen: my name is
"tango of the *Guadia Vieja*"
of a fame as long and even
as the Italian humbleness.
I've always taken drastic actions,
once and for all;
I'm the virile tango
driven into its *guardia vieja*
with a cigar on my ear
and a geranium between my teeth.

The rabble, saw from the very beginning
my sterling nature,
and, forming *media lunas* and *diques*,
danced to my rhythm.
My name is "don't feel daunted"
which is a good name,
I give myself to the one who knows
    how to give
without asking where and when:
I wasn't born to sing
because I was born to dance.

From the first steps
the guitars noticed me,
and the *taitas* understood me
tilting their hats.
Since the first steps
they told me about sex,
and to the rhythm of these raptures
I knew how to get it free:
I'm the *compadrón* tango
which wasn't born for fools.

If I'm to be described
I would tell you this:
a sterling *macho* man, good friend,
bad tempered dancer.
A strange-looking nighthawk,
tough, with a hard life,
full of himself with those who work
because he lives at other people's expense:
that's a man who
carries a knife in his belt.

He wears a neckerchief,
high-heeled shoes,
and checkered trousers
tight at the ankles.
A collarless shirt,
a lying-in-wait look,
short and straight jacket,
a tilted hat,
a rival in his head
and a chick in his heart.

That young creole woman
—so much criticized at the time—
who used to walk, take the streetcar
or a miserable carriage,
compared with today's girls, is a saint;
let me describe them:
naked to the waist,
a cigarette in their mouth
and a glass in their hand,
dancing with a friend.

Don't give me anything special
or so-called moneybags
with a few cents and manners
you can only see in the stories.
Don't give me anything special:
a maté, a black tobacco smoke;
a pimp who's hard up
because he spends everything he has,
an argentine chick
or an oriental party.

I face out the white-collar cops
and beat them
when my *malevo* look
makes its way with my knife.
If there are white-collar cops
I face them out;
and if they are fully-fledged *criollos*
we clash without trouble,
because while they are made of *quebracho*
my name is *ñandubay*.
And that's how I take it

without my fame running out,
with gray hair on my mustache
and my square long hair.
I feel upset and irritated when
I see those men who cry
on the corners for their chicks
with "bad boys" weeping:
in the past, the chicks' flight
was sorted out with a stick.

I finally say, fellows,
that today's tango bores me...
Get out of there... go...huh!
Tangos that taste like boleros...!
For tangos, the first ones,
until nineteen ten...
Those coming after
are songs with a taste of coke...
While the eau-de-vie is for the mouth,
tango is for the feet!

And now, flat broke
I live without making any racket;
as it is said in a refined language,
I have been "a sexual complex".
I must add that
I never fought in any gang;
I approached any kind of men,
curled hair, indian-looking or black guys:
that's why I never pay attention
to the team *guapo*.

And for the time being, brave young men,
I'll finish this *milonga*.
Tilting my *borsalino*
I'll head for my stop.
My "better than nothing"
    is waiting for me;
she's an excellent chick.
I'm the one who beats
when my mind is clear and when
    I'm drunk as well...
My hand is forbidden
but I still have my heart!

Fernando Quiñones

Chronicle of tango and the deceased little girl

At 3148 Chiclana street
where she lived with her father and mother
at 5.45 p.m.
and thirteen days before Christmas, in 1920,
this universal world ended for her
her permanent horrors and gifts
her fear of getting old which she still didn't have,
the nightmares and the light
     vanished;
the burning of the first kiss
disappeared from her saliva,
she had no memories, no bites
in her head and blood anymore
no more purplish dawns, wishing to
     come back home
no more gropes
no more laughs.
Pain and that fever that won't come down
went away as well:
     but yesterday night she seemed to be
     better
     the doctor came three times yesterday:
     when this point is reached, there's
     nothing we can do, be ready.

The prettiest in Chiclana
Meningitis
was 15 years old when she died
Estersita Dalto
Not Dalton, please
Dalto and a typical one:
D'Alto, sure.
More Italian than Spaventa and Di Stéfano
the little Italian girl
and today they call you Milonguita.
But now,
precisely the day of Gardel's 30th. birthday,
now the shadow is on top of you
now you come back
now *the declarant and*
     Cayetano Gorga,
     twenty two, single, who
     have seen the body fulfill their part

now the bandoneons burst
by themselves
Rivero is already extending his hands and
complaining,
a barge, as a dirty elegy, blows its bitter
     horn towards the Riachuelo
the horses in the racetrack remain
motionless
the secretary of Popular Education has
a bad suspicion.
Now you leave the neighborhood and tread on
the little story which is the great one.
Now everything is in order because the witnesses
     have already signed.
Now dust is covering you
with a perfectly serious knock of the coffin.

Immediately after we went to her house.

Roberto Arlt

The seven madmen

Alone

Alone...
Incredibly alone...!
I'm living the drama of waiting for you,
today...
tomorrow...
always the same.

Lyrics and music by Enrique Santos Discépolo
Enrique Santos Discépolo

Sometimes, itinerant musicians used to enter this lion's den, often a bandoneon and a guitar.

They tuned the instruments up and each beast curled up in its corner with an expectant silence, while sadness moved its invisible swell in that aquarium atmosphere.

The prison tango mournfully emerged from the soundboxes and then the scoundrels unconsciously made their resentment and misfortunes fit with the music. Silence was like a monster with many hands erecting a sound dome over the heads knocked down on marble. Perhaps that's what they were thinking about! And that terrible, tall dome that went deep into every chest, multiplied the guitar's and bandoneon's languor, deifying the whore's suffering and the jail's terrible boredom which pricks your heart when you think about your friends who are out putting even life at risk.

Then, an unknown tremor burst into the dirtiest souls, under the ugliest faces; later, everything was over and every single hand left a coin in the musicians' hat.

Una canción, *wash drawing by* Gabriel Di Toto.

Miguel D. Etchebarne

Juan Nadie, life and death of a "compadre"

He was born in a tin hut
facing a stream
which was an unfriendly snake
slipping away from one bush to another.
That water was pleasant
to his ephemeral innocence,
and on acquiring the experience
of a wild life,
he saw that only courage
keeps one's independence.

Through those poor vacant lots
crossed by the ditches,
he walked by fits and starts
during his first years;
he was raised like the *teros*
by the edge of the marshlands:
with his reddish wet feet,
his dry, injured mouth;
always looking for food
in birds and fishes.

The mother, as a slave,
kept her nose to the grindstone:
someone bled her dry
and on top of that, beat her.
(The father, of tough lineage,
died when Juan was born,
and he couldn't even see
his face on a photograph,
but felt his presence,
sometimes, when he suffered.)

He had a pretty elder sister
who was soon bitten.
Later, she left the area
looking for a better place.
He didn't hold a grudge against her
but didn't feel tenderness either:
he remembered her figure
as any other thing
and her skirt's passing
as a useless witeness.
That's how he gradually became an adult
without being one, among the burrs,
and at ten his eyes
shocked you as an insult.

He learned to dodge
every steady job;
he felt he was his own son
and the master of his future,
which he imagined to be unsafe
with intimate pleasure.

He felt death
in the bird's neck:
that warm soft death
which leaves the feather inert;
later he felt it more intensely
on slitting a foal's throat:
it hit him as a hammer
in the exposed arteries,
and shook him
in the knife handle.

He gradually got tougher
than the fin of a catfish,
quicker for the slap
and self-assured in pretending;
he could get out of a predicament
without help;
he spat the harsh words
and contained the friendly ones
and he only sensed in the rose
the naked woman.

Sadness followed him
as a woman in mourning:
he beat her like crazy
but she loved him anyway;
he used to be caught in the evening
holding on to her presence
and he, who had neither innocence
faith nor grace whatever,
sank in her wolfish shadow
as a memory in the absence.

He was born strong
and very unsociable
thin as a wick,
and wild as the wind;
hardening as a leather thong
under the frost and drizzle,
hurting himself with the barbed wire,

stealing both to the rich and poor,
he familiarized himself as a child
with card games and the picklock.

He lived in that scarce world
until, one day, for fun,
he knocked down, to give him fright,
an old man with a rubble.
A shiver ran down his spine
when he saw him fall;
later he felt that someone
ran while he escaped,
and without knowing if he was
     dreaming or not
he slept in the police station.

*The Maldonado stream and some of
its neighbors. 1883.*

An arrest on the bridge. 1912.

Anonymous lunfardo (circa 1890)

The other night at Los Corrales

Slaughterhouses, and, in the distance, the
garbage dump. 1890.

The other night at Los Corrales,
I discovered a very pretty *china*;
and right there, as if I was joking,
I began to moan at her.
I started to complain
and right there I made up a story
because on seeing the dough
I thought I could steal it from her.

But I was wrong:
she was a tough chick,
as wild as a beast
whose nest has been invaded;
and as I went too far,
farther than necessary,
she shouted a whole string
of unspeakable insults.

She started by saying that she had
an excellent pimp
and that she was not a dimwit
who could be robbed.
She said, do you think you can fool me
with such a cheap story?
I'm a cop's chick
and I will lock you up.

But since I get touchy
when I hear about jail,
I told her, nobody is robbing you
so stop feeling irritated.
And right there, I gave her a nice
scarf I had,
and asked her if she wanted
to leave the pimp.

She answered: it's impossible
but I don't want to spurn you;
the thing is I have a fool
I'm about to rob;
I'm about to see if the den
is all right because he's dumb;
and later, I will certainly
ditch him.

But I still want to know
If you're not deceiving me
and you have another chick with you
who's prettier than I am;
that's why I want to warn you
that I get very irritable
and I can't stand any other chick
around my love.

For that and other reasons,
I want you to tell me the truth,
in order to get rid of a fright
if the pimp shows up;
today he's coming to sleep
and it's very easy to imagine
that around half past eleven
he'll show up drunk in the den.

Then I told her
to tell the *madam*,
that she was thinking of
going to the inn to sleep with me;
and when her pimp comes
tell her to send him away,
that you're with someone else
and you can't open the door.

She settled everything with the *madam*,
we left the brothel together,
and went to an inn
where she asked for a room;
and around dawn
with my money and watch chain
the whore took flight
and left me in the room.
You should have seen me
mad at her for my money and watch chain!
To think I believed she
had swallowed my story...!
I got dressed, and went straight
to the brothel, to give her a hiding,
and the *madam* told me to
get out, you cheated fool.
Thus, as you can see, gentlemen,
can you imagine?
I really was
the dumb she had...!
I thought I had made up a good story,
but she took a flight first,
and stood me up so badly
as you can see.

This will set an example
to the swindler so that
he can choose a better environment
when he intends to rob;
he must be careful or what
recently happened to me
will happen to him too:
I had my dough and watch chain
stolen while I tried to be too clever by half.

José Portogalo

Letter for Juan Tango

Oh, café of those days
on Olavarría street,
where I used to turn up at nightfall
back in the year 1911...

When, in my suburb, I had
a reputation for being tough,
and Gardel was called "el morocho"
and Razzano "el Oriental".

Lyrics by Enrique Cadícamo
Music by Angel D'Agostino

Some people say it was in the streets
of the neighborhood of La Boca or Palermo;
others, in Los Corrales,
La Batería or San Telmo.
But, my friend, I believe
tango was born in the very
heart of Buenos Aires.
How? When? From where?
It doesn't matter; let them say
anything they want, but you must know
that it was born treading on stingin nettles,
sticking its chest out, self-assured,

with a star on its forehead
and a bird-like whistle.

....

It was rocked in the sheds
—with a dagger in its belt—;
it was danced by *"El Misto"* from Flores,
and Rosaura, *"La Ricura"*;
a guapo from Balvanera
fermented its yeast;
the Italian girl *"Carmelucha"*
caressed it in her skirt;

"El Vasco" Aín, in Europe,
unpicked its seams;
it was intertwined with the moon,
by *Pavura* and
"El Mosquito", on my sidewalk.
Chacarita, *"La Maleva"*,
"La Lora", Méndez, *"El Tarta"*
initialized it,
and so far, in my adolescence,
I added new luster to its dance
when I could barely spell
its name in my neighborhood.

A typical bar with its tough gang. 1910.

Raúl González Tuñón

The newspaper boys and dances at the Tabarís

—The newspaper boys were quite an institution, especially the boisterous and colorful group focused on the resale of the evening newspaper, at the workshop doors, in the streets, at the neighboring cafés. Among the newspaper vendors of all kinds, ranging from the great wholesaler to the simple resale laborer, from the person who was in charge of the distribution, to the street sparrow, there were many characters who were remarkable for their warmth and kindness. I especially remember Arístides Gutiérrez, nicknamed *El gordito Liceo,* because when he was a boy, before becoming a distributor, he sold newspapers at the corner of that theater; *El Ruso Lima*, who got that nickname because he a was red-haired boy and had sold his newspapers on the corner of Avenida de Mayo and Lima street; the small and big *Panchiquitos* brothers; the *Milonga* and *Milonguita* brothers; *El Dotor de Boedo*, who later became a theater producer; *El Rana, Madre, Sopo, Trompa de Hacha, Sábalo, Pelito Verde, Manolo Monteagudo*, and many others. They loved us a lot and we loved and respected them. It was mutual, you know... When, in 1928, Enrique and I won municipal awards, a great banquet was held in our honor, with speeches, a poetry reading and, at the end, a share out of Santos cigars. What a party! We ended up at the Tabarís.

—*Did you dance often?*

—Yes we did, but not only tango. That's why, after the banquets, as that of the newspaper boys, we used to go to the Tabarís. Oliverio and Güiraldes thoroughly enjoyed it. Güiraldes got always a box, we ordered champagne and I used to dance with Norah Lange. In those days, you know, Marechal and I were rivals. There was often rivalry between us to dance tango. I think I danced better than he did. But since he is dead, I take back what I said, because he cannot contradict me.

Newspaper boys. c.1918.

Bernardo Verbitsky

The success
of a singer

—I'm not going to be paid and on top of that I have to pay the accompaniment. It's unbelievable— said Tito summarizing his reasons for rejecting the invitation.

The whole gang contradicted him. He couldn't miss the opportunity to perform in public. The Boedo's café was a fine place with a first-rate orchestra whose debut was embellished that way. The invitation was due to a concatenation of relationships but even so, it proved that his name was circulating and that it was worth trying to consolidate it before a large audience. The presence of several well-known musicians, among whom a number of conductors, would offer a unique opportunity. Others had started a career in similar circumstances. And, of course, the applause was guaranteed. They promised. That's why, in no way could he refuse that invitation.

—I've got—, said Raúl who had just joined the group, —some great gossip to tell you. Pichuco is going to be there. The other singer of his orchestra feels overwhelmed by Edmundo Rivero's success and voice, and he has already said he's leaving, and Troilo is looking for a replacement. If only he could listen to you, and...

—And he's going to choose me. You're crazy

Tito put special emphasis on the detail of payment. He was not willing, for the pleasure of showing himself, to spend a sum he didn't have.

And he repeated with determination:

—I'm not going.

—You're not going because of the money? What do you think?— asked Luis as if he was speaking in a court of justice.

The young man's answer was simple. They put their hands in their pockets and in two minutes, they got the money; they could even have raised twice the amount they needed since they all worked and had saved a few pesos. Tito tried to look offended, but he couldn't refuse anymore. At first, he questioned that contribution which he had not asked for, but the others were glad to be of help and in the same expeditious way they had raised the money he needed, they forced him to accept it, attracting the attention of everybody at the café who did not understand what was going on. They all went to Boedo, of

Opening Session of the Academia Nacional del Tango, with the presence of Natalio Etchegaray, Ricardo Bellini, Horacio Salas, Horacio Ferrer, Julio Bárbaro and Jorge Faruk. The Golden Hall at the Colón Theater, June 30, 1990.

Pichuco by Víctor Sassón.

The Aníbal Troilo Orchestra, performance broadcasted on Belgrano radio station.

course, and their applause contributed to highlight Tito's success. In fact, in lieu of one or two songs, he had to sing four, in all the enthusiasm, supported by his friends.

Troilo didn't show up, and Tito preferred not to find out if this had been made up by Raúl. But the author of the lyrics of one of the tangos included in the repertoire of the orchestra which was making its stage debut, who had good connections with a popular radio, managed to persuade them that night, to go over to the café so that the concert could be broadcasted —as an announcer put it- "all over the ether— Tito knew later that most of his neighborhood had listened to him on that occasion and that his voice had even reached his home's radio. His mother told him that the old man didn't go to sleep at the usual time and, although he pretended to read his newspaper, as he usually did after dinner, he remained near the radio all the time. And although nobody managed to get an opinion from him or to make him confess he had listened to the radio, the episode had a second repercussion at home. There were some photos of the café's party in a magazine in which Tito stood out clearly. Joaquín showed the magazine to his sister Celia in front of his father who didn't take the hint, not even when the girl remarked that Tito looked just like his father in that photo, something that, was absolutely true. Later, Celia told Tito she had seen their father, when he thought he was alone, put on his glasses in order to furtively examine the magazine's pictures.

A few days later, he was asked to perform in some "tribute" to a neighbor of Forest Avenue —that was the only information he got— which later turned out to be a "charity" performance even if he couldn't find out for whom. A complete disorder reigned during the performance, something which prevented Tito from excelling himself who, in addition, had to pay for the guitarists out of his own pocket since he didn't want the guys to pay the expenses again. All these steps, the search for an accompaniment, public performances, and his hopes of being called by one of the radios, made him sink into a state of agitation which even affected his friends. All of them slept less hours. Tito was sometimes off work during these two weeks.

Conde Hermann von Keyserling

South American meditations

Tango. This dance was born in ambiguous suburbs and its more important precedents were the black cuban dances and the neapolitan songs. Given the great passivity of the Argentine nature, it is obvious that the stimulus had to come from abroad. But the limitless and hopeless immensity, melancholy and passion of Argentina were soon expressed through the borrowed forms, in the same way that the english spirit creatively changed the primitive germanic-romance jargon into a convincing original language. The black-neapolitan sluggishness was replaced by the firm broncobuster's moderation. The riding crop lash, adapted to the guitar, created a masculine rhythm. Nowadays, tango belongs, as a

Miguel A. D'arienzo: Tango del Vaticano, *oil painting. (Zurbarán Collection).*

music and dance, to the classicism of the time. The way the *compadritos* dance it —the only authentic way from the historical point of view— is already seen as a sacrilege, although, around 1900, there was hardly another way of dancing it.

You can say the same thing with regard to the voluptuous way in which it is danced in Europe. With a proper interpretation, tango does not express a free passion but a suspended one, in the same way as the *Río de la Plata* carries the red sand suspended in its waters to the sea. Tango is fairly similar to the minuet; it's just that the latter is the expression of an autumnal melancholy and the former expresses the melancholy of spring.

Hagan círculo, *an oil painting by Juan Carlos Benítez (detail).*

Waldo Frank

A symphony
of forms

In the heart of the tango we find the black man, that with the domain of his master's music, has won a sweet and profound revenge. The tom-tom of the African forests, is a deep beat, weak but accurate. A beat that is like a seed that grows in the substance of the song, and the seed like a spark that lights the whole body of the music; however, the dance is kept hard as the seed and wild as the tom-tom. The whole human eloquence from Andalucía, that is a symphony of forms, is in the body of the tango, and the open path of the pampa is also there.

The tango is a march in which the vertical ecstasy from Spain is stratified in a horizontal step, where the assault of the plainsman is held back in an elevated reservation in which both, Spain and the pampa, get together in the same stroke of blood.

The black men, with their marimbas over the splendor of the bonfire, are the rhythm; the trot of the gauchos, the lyrics and the heroic union of dreams and bravery of Spain, the soft musical phrase.

The men and women dancers in the underground saloon are poor human samples. The men dress in cheap suits, they have livid eyes and their heads very brilliantly combed. The women use humble Paris styled imitations and wear very high healed shoes that hold long thin legs. But they become ennobled when they walk in the tango. The man leads their long steps, fainted, flexible. His body is straight, it does not bend; the head is kept sideways in relation to his body, and pushed against the face, also sideways, of the woman. Even the hands appear smashed and, when the couple turns and the plastically united bodies move together slowly, not a muscle nor any part of their bodies, break the union of the connection. The effect is strictly sculptural. The world is a solid element that turns, goes up and down; the world is the music and the dancers a substantial lengthening of this world. But its cautious step – a natural effort deliciously turned into art, like the effort of sexual love – transforms this world, it makes it immovable and gives compass to its flow.

Within the pure outline of the tango figures roars the desire for sex. The bodies don't touch each other; although, they are together. The stream between the man and the woman is so intense, that it bounces from one to the other, and it processes them. This sexual blue mist is also in touch with the music, that is the substance of life itself, because, within it, are the pampa, the altar and the jungle. Therefore sex is not excluded from the world, the electrical shock of desire between the dancing bodies is caught in the continuity in the song of the world and the tangent of the song are dominated by the severe steps of the dancers.

The tango is the world's most profound popular dance. The Terpsichore genius of three eminent plastic races, the blacks, the Indian and the Spanish, have gender it. Nevertheless, it is essentially modern and particular of the porteño; and so intimately personal as the body of the woman that dances it. In its voice is the breath that sings it; the sweet gracefulness of its form requires its delicious serenity; and in her large eyes the lustful desire and the spirit of Christ, that the tango must resolve.

Man is the creator of the dance because it genders over the woman's body.

La guitarra en el ropero, *painting by Vicente Forte.*

Bailarines de tango, 1900, *painting by Sigfredo Pastor.*

Mural painting by the Grupo Cambalache, which is a tribute to Hugo del Carril, opposite the Flores Station of the Sarmiento Railway.

About critics and detractors

Tango, as a cultural phenomenon, had tenacious opponents. Its origins, which emerged from brothels, contributed to forge a distorted view and many Argentine intellectuals were quick to distance themselves from it with the aim of preventing any kind of contamination. And in this list, there are some right-wing authors, such as Lugones and Ibarguren, or left-wing writers, such as Leónidas Barletta or Ezequiel Martínez Estrada.

Tango is a jeremiad of effeminate persons, a late awakening of a woman unaware of her femininity. It is the music of some degenerates who refuse to wear proletarian clothes, whose greasy-haired women leave the factories for the brothels... Tango is unhealthy. The sensuality that prevails in it emerges from inhibition, shyness and fear. The music of other nations is quite sensual, cleverly sexual. In tango, sensuality is something false, artificially created.

Leónidas Barletta

It is the dance from the waist down. From the waist up, the body does not dance; it goes stiff, as if the awake legs were carrying two bodies that have gone to sleep in a hug. Its merit, as that of marriage, lies in the daily routine, in what is usual, with no starts whatever.

An expressionless, monotonous dance, with the town hall's stylized rhythm. It lacks, unlike the other dances, a meaning focused on the senses, with its plastic language, so stimulating, or capable of arousing related movements in the audience's soul, through happiness, enthusiasm, admiration or desire. It's a dance without soul, made for automatons, for persons who have given up the complications of their mental life or have turned to nirvana. It's like gliding. A dance of pessimism, of every limb's sorrow; a dance of the large wide plains and of a weighed down, subjugated race which goes all over them aimlessly, without destination, in the eternity of its present which repeats itself. Melancholy comes from that repetition, the contrast resulting from seeing two bodies organized for free movements which have been submitted to the biggest animal's mechanical walking. I feel sorry for those young horses with the spindle.

Ezequiel Martínez Estrada

Mayoral and Elsa María: dancing with elegance.

An illegitimate product, which neither has the wild fragrance, nor the natural grace of the land, but the sensual style of the suburbs, has gone all over the world delighting the motley guests of the european hotels and the habitués of the cafés in the large capital cities: tango, a so-called hallmark of the argentine people which has been wrongly given by the whole world. In fact, tango is not exactly an argentine product; it is a hybrid or half-caste product, which was born on the suburbs and is a mixture of tropical *habanera* and forged milonga. What a difference between tango's harsh swinging and the noble and distinguished cueca, which shows the same aristocratic expression as a pavane or a minuet!

Carlos Ibarguren

If you are able to appreciate people's spirit through music; if the latter is, as I believe, the most genuine revelation of those people's character, the *gaucho* stands out in it. The elegant spirit of its compositions, its light grace, its sentimental refinement, defines today's creole music, anticipating its future. In that swift structure lies the secret of its superior fate, not in the contortions of tango, that brothel's reptile, so unfairly labeled as Argentine at the time of its shameless vogue. The powerful predominance of rhythm in our dances is, I repeat, a virile condition which carries the foetus' vital flair. The couple's corporal separation is possible and fine-looking thanks to the rhythm which thus controls the pantomime, in lieu of being its rogue, as it happens with tango music, only appointed to make the movements fit in with the provocative wiggle, the equivocal reluctance of the embrace, which tightness is demanded by the dance, thus defining its true character.

Leopoldo Lugones

Bailongo, *ink by Fernando Guibert.*

Marcelino del Mazo

Tango dancers

When the rhythm of that tango indicated them a bar rest
as serpents inspired by a breath of passion,
they interwove... And they were segments of a strange bloomed
creeper showered by the hall's comments.
—Now, baby!— howled the *compadre* and his wild partner
offered the impudence of her warm shamelessness,
reaching with her flesh as a tongue of fire,
the vibratile bowels of that naughty lover.
They spun round; the violins caused quite a commotion
and the flute uttered some notes nobody has ever written.
But the dancers moved softly, to the beat of the music,
and the intoxicated couple kissed, without realizing...

Astor Piazzolla, the "bandoneonista" boy.

Carlos de la Púa

Old tango

Macho dance, excellent and fond of parties,
malevo and pretentious, indecent dance,
carrying in the suburban spin
the cadence of *candombe* origin,
as an old and filthy film.
Passion of chicks of low lineage,
for whom you are life's anger,
a whim with the feeling of a slit,
when a corte breaks them like a slice,
or their skin gets confused by a run.
Despicable and *porteño* gossip
that acts in bad faith,
brave, daring, skittish compliment,
acting as a support and a pimp,
heading towards the wild side.
He who dances you well must be shrewd,
well-known among the *guapos'* gang,
must have done a picklock job
and a jail feeling
faced with the atavistic influence of clothes.

Carlos Vega

Argentine dances and songs

Tango faced, during its first years, somber forecasts. Its immediate death was announced time and time again. Today, in the presence of the triumphant dance, people laugh at those early predictions. And there's nothing to laugh at. If tango is that broken, nervous and lively music; that of the *corte* and the *quebrada*; that of a limpid and stressed rhythm, everything turned up as it was predicted. In modern tango, nothing of the primitive creole tango remains. It evolved with the objective of saving itself.

Julio Bocca dances accompanied by the Orquesta Sinfónica Nacional. 1998.

Horacio Salas

The dance: history of passion

Since far-off times, the dance has been an essential element to tango and it has also been a key factor to its widespread dissemination all over the world. A sensual and focused dance, severe and nostalgic, which influence still reaches the farthest corners of the planet. From the little primitive tango, a direct heir to *candombe*, to the turn of the century —*tango picado*, the 1920s— and 1930s, walking tango and some current exaggerated contortions, the dance has covered a long way in its evolution. When a veteran tango lover watches certain absorbed couples, counting the steps and tirelessly practicing rehearsed figures, he often smiles with a certain warm disdain in view of this affected rigor from some young dancers who pay more attention to the remarks of a pro-

fessor than to the impulse of rhythm. Benito Bianquet, better known as "El Cachafaz", used to say that tango figures should respond to improvisation, where the dancers are carried, as Jorge Luis Borges said in *Hombre de la esquina rosada*, 'by the tide of tango'. A dance where the couple's conversation is not allowed since the dancers must be focused on the music swing and the invitations drawn by the figures. Juan Carlos Copes, one of the most important names in tango dance, holds that tango "depends on each one's inspiration; it must be danced right down the floor, without trying to jump along, because that's not tango". Another myth of tango dance, "Virulazo", said one day that tango 'in a nutshell, is nothing but walking for some minutes, to the rhythm of the orchestra, holding a woman who knows how to answer to each of the man's intentions. The rest is gymnastics'. However, the new generations, as expected, have added their own criteria and created a tango which allows stylization and shows a somewhat theatrical choreography, similar to ballet standards. Perhaps because this dance offers, ever since its birth, a wide range of possibilities, all the way from hypnotism, seduction, to conquest.

The genesis of the dance

But tango as a dance recognizes a history which genesis plunges into the mysteries surrounding any myth. It is known that in the days following Caseros, a battle marking the fall of dictator Juan Manuel de Rosas and the early stages of the modern Argentina, the Cuban habanera, brought by the sailors covering the trade route between the Caribbean ports and the Río de la Plata, took root on the outskirts of Buenos Aires and Montevideo. The *habanera*, already under influence of Spanish rhythms, on arriving in this region of the world, was soon combined with the *milonga*, a heir to the old *payada*.

A spontaneous poetry from the Uruguayan countryside and the province of Buenos Aires, on arriving in the suburbs, the *payada* turned into milonga. In its classic work, *Cosas de negros*, Vicente Rossi defined: "The *milonga* is the small-town payada. Its octosyllabic verses are recited with a certain pleasant tone, colored with some proper guitar interventions, filling the bar rests between strophes with a characteristic three-tone plucking, while the milonguero breathes heavily or takes his breath. It turns into song when the improvisations kept in the popular memory are recited; it is payada when improvised. The *payadores*' classic used to have six verses; that of the *milongueros*, four".

According to lexicologist José Gobello, *milonga* is a word in quimbunda language, which means "word": the word of the payadores. In 1872, when José Hernández published the first part of his *Martín Fierro*, the word had already acquired the meaning of "getting toget-

her in a dance": *"I learned once, unfortunately, /there was a dance somewhere, / and half desperate / I went to the milonga"*.

Ten years later, the milonga was the popular dance par excellence. Ventura Lynch reported in 1883: *"On the outskirts of the city, the* milonga *is so widespread that it is a required piece in every low-class little dance, and is played on guitar, accordion, a comb with a piece of paper and by traveling flutists, harpists and violinists. Its also played by organists who have arranged it and play it with a* habanera *air. The latter is also danced in riffraff casinos located in the* "11 de Septiembre" *and* "Constitución" *markets, as well as in dance halls and get together"*.

According to Rossi, the dance development, with no tango characteristics yet, took place in the *"chinas*' rooms": *"The rooms occupied by the women near the barracks, on both sides of the Río de la Plata, were called like that. These women were black,* mulatas, *aboriginal and of mixed race, and some of them were also white. When the soldiers were on leave, some entertaining and noisy parties took place in those rooms (...) civilians, hardened men from the suburbs and some friends of the house also used to attend; the presence of musicians and singers was always very welcome, because such gatherings were hardly conceived without music, songs and a "little turn". When the notes of the* milonga *or estilo went around the neighborhood, the residents who were still in good harmony with the owner of the room where the party was held, turned up to* "give it brilliance"; *invariably, the temptation to* "give it a spin" *was impossible to resist, and the dance started with the efficient assistance of an accordion, the favorite instrument for these occasions which was skillfully handled by some* criollos(...). *People danced by couples, man and woman held each other, as in the society's dances, a style which was also called* à la française, *since this custom was supposed to come from Paris; but the first thing that struck your attention was the different techniques used by the family or "society" couples and those couples coming from the suburbs. In the first case, the bodies did not touch themselves, and the man was the one who*

Dancing in the street.
Caminito. La Boca.

moved back. On the other hand, the lower-class couples danced exactly the other way around: the bodies came into more or less a contact, according to the couple's closeness; the woman always moved back; with no contortions or stumbles, "straight ahead", in "the decent way". The corte *and the* quebrada *had not appeared yet".* And Rossi continues: *"The favorite (in those cases) was the* danza, *of african-west Indian origins, which was taken to their country by the French in the Can-Can period, due to its soft and serene sensuality which compensated the latter's furious lightness (...). Later, our suburban dancer subdued this* danza *which was brought here by cuban sailors to his artistic and bold ways. Its second name (that of* Habanera) *emerged from its origin; gradually, our suburban dancer transformed the* habanera *(...).*

The dancing parties in the "chinas' rooms" were immediately visited by the Danza, as it came from the port neighborhoods, and when largely dominated and changed into a creole dance, it became a must in the lively suburban parties. The third name defined its new transformation and it was called milonga, *through a logical and natural process: its little dances extended a singing session or, as it was said and is still said today, people proceeded to* milonguear. *This kind of parties was then called* milonga; *therefore,* 'let's go to a milonga' *could mean either* 'let's go sing' o 'let's go dance', *or both. The tempting and new dance could not avoid the holy oil of the environment where it* was created and was called milonga *and then incorporated into a clear creole expression."*

On June 6, 1880, Benigno B. Lugones explained in *La Nación* that the quadrille, the lanciers, the contredance, the minuet and, in general, every dance danced by separate couples could be accepted and was still accepted in high society's milieus. *"But the polka, the mazurka, the waltz and some other pieces are banned from decent ball halls (the habanera, Scottish, danza) are the highest abomination."*

Gobello holds that tango is the mazurka's and *milonga*'s africanization, and that its origin was not an individual dance, but merely a different way of dancing rhythms already well-known.

There is almost no doubt that —as Ventura Lynch said in his work *La provincia de Buenos Aires hasta la definición de la cuestión capital (Buenos Aires, 1883)*— the milonga as a dance was created by the compadritos to make fun of the dances held by black people in their "places". At the beginning, the couples danced it separately, as in the camdombe; later, it turned into a dance with an embraced couple, preferably men, until it reached the brothels. In 1903, *Caras y Caretas* magazine still published a series of slightly sardonic photographs where you could see two suburban dancers in a street scene, rehearsing tango figures.

This seems to be true, but one must not exaggerate: the dance was also accepted by mixed couples. In 1889, three years after the performance of *Juan Moreira*, a drama by Eduardo Gutiérrez, as a pantomime, in the performance by the circus of the Podestá brothers one could see mixed couples dancing a *milonga*. This dance was performed in the final scene, which takes place in a brothel where *Sergeant Chirino* takes *Moreira* by surprise and kills him from behind when the latter tries to escape. On the previous dance, you could see some couples performing simple steps, suitable for the family. Even the Bates brothers say that this music was especially written for Antonio Podestá's work, with the title, *La estrella.*

Musicologist Néstor Ortiz Oderigo has pointed out that, in its choreographic origins, tango was not performed by an embraced couple, but was a pelvic dance, where a woman and a man faced each other in order to perform different movements, mime, and figures, clearly influenced by the *candombe*. With the intention of strengthening his thesis, he notes that in an engraving in *La Ilustración Argentina* magazine, on November 30, 1882, there is a black couple dancing face to face, and the epigraph reads: "The tango".

Biography of an embrace

Carlos Vega has a different opinion. The figures of tango recognize for him a different influence in their origins: *"From the choreographic point of view, tango is a real finding. The porteño creators, who did not resign themselves to perpetuating anodyne walking steps and talkative turns which every dance performed by an embraced couple was led to, had tried some innovations in the performance of those same dances, the milonga and even the quadrille".* And he continues: *"The Argentine tango performs the miracle of inserting the figure into the embrace, that is to say, tradition into innovation. That's the secret of its success; that's the main innovation it offers to the world.'* And he adds: *'The prevailing dances with embraced couples demanded the 'constant movement', according to the established practices: the dancing couple had to link rhythmic steps or turns without stopping for a minute. Now, the creators of tango bring in the suspension of movement. The couple suddenly stays motionless. In fact, the man is the one who stops while the woman turns around and, the other way around, the woman stays still, and the man moves. It does not seem much, but sometimes a sensational finding is the sum of trifling things".* Vega also says: *"The dancers had posed the simple dilemma: either we squeeze together or we tread on each other. And they squeezed together. With no lust whatever; the critics were those who introduced lust in tango. The dancers had a lot of things to think of. They danced for the pleasure of dancing, but they danced fighting. The rivalry between the dancers, the struggle between the neighborhoods, were the center of attention and required to be very careful. The*

man could not move back while he danced, as required by courtesy, because he could not turn his back to a potential enemy. An attack from behind was an exceptional, but not impossible, event. A defeated rival could have stood up looking for revenge. Every man in the world moves forward on dancing due to a porteño *distrust".*

The fact is that by mid-1890s, tango had its own choreography, which was consolidated at the turn of the century.

The Folklore Ballet dances to the compass of the "Juan de Dios Filiberto" Argentine National Orchestra in the National Culture Feast, 1998.

The suburban man was proud to be a good dancer. Being a "bad dancer" could be as negative for his virile prestige as being clumsy with the knife. Even such a controversial character as Ecuménico López, protagonist of *Un guapo del 900* by Samuel Eichelbaum (a play from which Leopoldo Torre Nilsson made a memorable film starring Alfredo Alcón) knows —without showing any *compadrito* trait, though— how to excel at tango. Nobody could make an impact without knowing its main figures. One also went to dance in the brothel.

During the first decade of this century, already consolidated as a music and choreography, tango began to leave behind the suburban low-class dance halls to go downtown. There were several dance places at the time, such as *"Lo de maría la Vasca"* and *"Lo de Laura"* and, in addition, people kept dancing in the brothels. For the upper-class men, the practice of tango figures was a *macho* prank, and with this criterion some young men from the high society of Buenos Aires brought the dance to Europe, where between 1911 and 1914, tango was all the rage.

In the neighborhoods and the patios of the tenement houses, the humble family men disapproved of daughters dancing that music of sinful lineage, and they only allowed it when the *compadritos* themselves turned it more decent. Thus, they created a special choreography, which was called the "tango of the sisters", that is to say, which could be danced with the family women, neither with *cortes, quebradas*, nor the figures that could remind the low origins of the dance.

In the late 1920s, the music became slower and lilting and less rhythmic than in its early stages; likewise, the dance lost its initial brothel connotations. The dancers performed according to a walking pattern, and adopted a less lively and almost melancholic choreography. Hence the phrase by Discépolo about *"the sad thought which can be danced"*. Thanks to this choreography which was allowed to be performed at the family homes and in the lofty dance halls, tango was a big success in every social class. This huge popularity reached its highest point during the 1940s, in hundreds of clubs and other entertainment places.

In mid-1950s, tango declined in the popular taste and the dance began to lose its popularity as well, only to be recovered in recent times through the most varied cinematic output in the world. And in this recovery, as I said before, the old erotic aspects of the early stages of tango appeared once again. A more thoughtful, interpreted, rehearsed and less improvised tango, but without losing its concentrated air which made it famous all over the world.

León Benarós

Arolas

A bandoneon baptized him.
He belonged to that group of young men
who, with one *taquito* and one *sentada*
used to shave the floor.
He did with tango everything he wanted;
the guitars sang for him
we cried all by ourselves for him...
May I have your attention, fellows;
please take your hats off:
I'm talking about Arolas!

Tall, thin and pale,
wearing borderline trousers,
a tilted hat
and with tango in his heart,
he got into the bandoneon
at the corner bar
and, to the rhythm of *chamuchina*
on the polished floors
he saw the patent leather
shoes shine.

If some little old organ
goes past the suburb
or someone whistles,
the tango *Derecho viejo*,
a milonguero prayer
sends a shiver down our spine
and a suburban requiem
trembles in the lonely streets:
they are praying for Arolas
and we must take our hats off.

Osvaldo Piro and his bandoneón.

Gardel

The porteño presence

Carlos Gardel, *caricature by*
Hermenegildo Sábat.

Máximo Paz,
Retrato de Gardel,
tempera.

Florencio Escardó

The persistence of the porteño sentimentalism

Carlos Gardel is the only true persistent feeling in Buenos Aires' sentimentalism. It is an unquestionable fact which has often been denied, but must be recognized when one truly faces without apriorisms the porteño reality; in addition, it is a fact which comprises every social class; the portrait of "Carlitos" is stuck on almost every truck windshield and on the walls of grocery stores and bootblacks shops, but it is also true that his records are played in the houses of the middle class and are praised by everybody as a result of the true and natural *porteño* tendency. This very intense and broad phenomenon, goes beyond a mere admiration for the star, the difficult attraction to the successful artist or the female's liking to the handsome singer. Carlos Gardel represents a level of coincidence and harmony obvious enough to see in it a more intimate and true cause than a lucky success. In fact, Carlos Gardel's figure goes beyond the Capital city and extends to the whole territory of the Republic; however, it is an essentially porteño fact. Because you can find in Gardel several characteristics of Buenos Aires which produce a combination of effects never caused by any other man before, precisely the ones most valued and better liked by the porteño. No doubt there is a series of different circumstances which have efficiently contributed to the creation of the symbol —e.g. his tragic death like something out of a novel— but of course the symbol was in him in a particularly propitious way.

Before starting its analysis, we would like to point out we do not intend here to heap praises upon this symbol, but simply to gather up the elements with the intention of giving a diagnosis; but we are not going to deny a certain liking for this work; a liking for a man whose name and voice make the beloved city smile.

Carlos Gardel shows many things which belong to the *porteño*. First, his origin; nobody knows it well, it is said he is french; others hold he is from Uruguay; perhaps he was born in

La sonrisa de Gardel, *oil painting by Alfredo Plank.*

Entre Ríos, and, besides, is Gardel his real name? It doesn't matter, being porteño is not an affiliation, it's a presence; what can we say? He is there, his name is already well-known, and he is *porteño*. It's enough. On the other hand, Carlos Gardel dresses with great care, almost in an affected way, and if he shows some affectation, it's something natural. Just what the *porteño* adores. You may not be simple, but you must be careful not to show affectation, that's his formula. Carlitos certainly doesn't think he is a sort of national hero, since everybody feels him close; everyone feels like talking to him, questioning him or demanding him; perhaps nobody really does it, but the *porteño* guesses he can do it and what more could he ask for? This is also a fundamental condition for deserving his intense affection. Gardel is very popular, but the city that allows him to be successful does not admire the splendor of his success, but his toughness in the road, his persistence in the effort, and a total lack of improvisation; the city knows he has worked in second-rate theaters and cafés, movie theaters and parties, he had to fight hard to get on in his way to success, but, in addition, he doesn't let it show. The porteño audience is not fond of heroes; for Gardel, success — which is hard to attain, and he knows it— is something easy, natural, and light. On the other hand, Gardel does not bring a significant message, a messianic plan, a cultural work; he does not come to employ people, but to give free rein to a deep sentimentalism, to show at a hedonist level an expressive song; and at this level, you may find the intellectual and the worker, the doctor and the ignorant, the teenager and the old man, and, above all, the woman, a melodious being par excellence.

The city feels it has been transfused in Gardel, because it loves in him, first the song, then, tango. The song and its peculiar form, tango, are for the *porteño* two kinds of a repressed effusiveness and it feels Gardel is the character who expresses them and frees them.

LE TANGO DE
CARLOS GARDEL

*Catalogue of the exhibition at the City Library of
Toulouse, in november 1984. Painting by
Hermenegildo Sábat.*

Pedro Orgambide

Symbolism

Gardel's perennial smile, as the Gioconda's, has a meaning. Besides being an acting tic (as it certainly is), it emphasizes the character's successful reality. As a symbolism, it represents the friendly Argentine of the 1920s. The one of prosperity, who doesn't feel disturbed by the "working-class bad mood". Who is both apocalyptic and a follower of the government's policies. Gardel is his mirror, his symbol. Other satellites of popular devotion revolve around him, such as Leguisamo himself *(Leguisamo solo! Viejo y peludo nomás!)* with the festive atmosphere of the racetrack, the guys shouting from the grandstands, the excitement of a breathtaking finish to a race in the Palermo racetrack. The turf, tango. The democratic racetrack (that of the *ñatos*, the *pibes* of the popular seats) meets —through Gardel— the turn-of-the-century aristocratic racetrack, described by the 1880s reporters or by César Duayen (Emma de la Barra) in *Stella*. Top hats and espadrilles. Presidents, ministers who go to the racetrack (and to the shows of the Sociedad Rural) by carriage but who are also frequently seen with jockeys and tango singers. These are the first signs of an oligarchic populism which, from the 1930s, is going to become established. Gardel smiles. It is not a question of being for or against him. Coexistence, agreement, connivance. Both Argentinas juxtaposed: that of the strikers and the tenement houses and that of the *Corso de la Flores* on the *Avenida de las Palmeras* in the neighborhood of Palermo. Anarchists in Puerto Nuevo and, further away, the guys are having fun at the *Parque Japonés,* with the roller coaster and the *looping the loop.* Gardel smiles to everybody. He belongs to everyone. Beyond contradiction. Bourgeois or populist. As tango.

To get a *"high social"* standing in the 1920s-Argentine social structure, was the project of many *criollos* and immigrant sons. But how could they reach such a social standing? The effort of a working father who, after an exhausting working week, made his house on sundays, did not seem the right way. Easy money (which several decades later would be called *sweet money)* did not come from the work-salary relationship, including the surplus value. *Get away from work, don't work for the smart guys*, suggested the tango *Seguí mi consejo*

On the Figueroa Alcorta Avenue, an allegory about the porteño myths, painted by Carlos Páez Vilaró.

(1928) with music by Salvador Merico and lyrics by Eduardo Trongué. The proposal (the seduction) focused on learning a new code, which could be copied, at least in its outside aspects, by the bourgeoisie from the high class: *...sleep on a feather mattress/ eat with champagne/ sleep twelve hours while the sun is still up/ eat your stew in the old Tropezón/ be a good a friend of whisky...etc.* This magic adaptation, this simulation of a certain behavior (...a smart man doesn't go to work) leaves out a significant detail: the possession of money, of enough resources to change from one social class to another. According to tango's advice, you only have to imitate a behavior, which is the consequence of and not the condition for gaining access to this transformation. This tanguistic poetic license describes well the hedonistic fantasy of the poor who continued to work for the *"smart guys"*. In the meantime, from the very center of contradiction, the tango with a social intention emerged, and would also be sung by Gardel.

Celedonio Flores

Carlos Gardel

Héctor Yánover

Buenos Aires

I don't want to play the role of a bard, or be
called an apologist by people:
I just want to tell the truth,
and that truth, buddy, is obvious.
Because if you have class and feelings
and you listen to Carlitos boastfully singing
there is no verse, no discourse, no feeling,
for the noble, honest and sincere praise.
He is a thrush, he's a canary, he's harmony
the milonga in the flesh, he's poetry,
that which emerges from the sweetness of his songs.
And on listening to him, other bards let out a yell,
swear and are green with envy,
and tie their pants up with wire.

The shadow of Gardel slips away through the walls
where there are torn posters announcing old dances.
The rain has slowly stained
with dirty spots a time of knives.

The year nineteen thirty wears the nuptial crepes
of a Buenos Aires which is all bride of a day
and in the splendor of its old songs
shadows lie on the mythology.

And we look at the mummies,
we discover the graves,
Betinotti, Gabino, the murderers
and all those stars who went away with time.

We are and we are not their sons. The venerable beard
of the soul, forces us to rethink everything.
And on the corner which was before the lout by trade
everybody sighs by the beloved tango.

Buenos Aires starts every day
and doesn't want to forget its past and it forgets it
because if it has a past it's almost nothing
as opposed to the vast life proposed by the future.

Alberto Girri

Memory of Gardel

"El mundo es y será...", *graphite by Ricardo Carpani.*

On declining his devoted throat
the last stretch,
the art of calmly preparing,
the rough and desolated natural death,
it was like a challenge thrown out to the markets,
the hidden, inaccessible story,
by the obscure people without pomp.
And the fact is that in the middle of the autumn,
people began to see him day after day
surviving in the honeysuckles,
standing by the constant streetlight;
and so many words, so much breath,
were only good for oblivion,
which often pours out flowers
and heaves sighs

in the unsociable poor of the suburbs,
in the glosses of the betrayed men,
in short, in everything which is tired of running
which flows, declines, ceases,
in the memories of the beloved river.
But the city knows a lot of him and keeps
his most rich tear, his harm which suddenly injured
the hidden boastfulness, the silent coolness,
with which the voices which remain silent,
around smoking chairs and dawns,
are accustomed to say affections to each other.
And maybe because I'm one of those,
I feel embarrassed about repeating the name,
getting tied up with the despicable temporary nostalgia
for claiming him.

Humberto Costantini

Gardel

Memoria de Gardel, *collage by Natalia Cohen.*

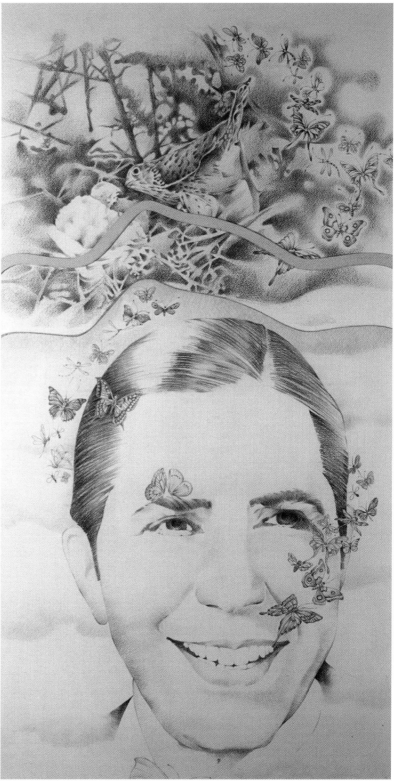

In my opinion, we invented him.
It possibly happened on a sunday afternoon,
    with *mate,*
    with memories,
    with sadness,
with a very soft music, on the radio,
after the football matches.
A photo on the wall probably distressed us,
some "I don't want to",
some book.
I think we probably were like that,
bored stiff,
remembering some solitary "what for",
with neither woman nor money,
and dull.
We suddenly felt
very lonely,
very orphan, like children.
Perhaps we were at rock bottom.
Perhaps somebody thought about killing himself.
Then, I don't know,
something very strange happened to us.
A sort of angel came from inside us,
we became prophetic
we woke up biblical.
We looked at the spiderwebs of the ceiling,
and said to ourselves:
"Let's make a God similar
to what we wanted to be and couldn't be.
Let's leave him the best,
the dreamy and bird part
of ourselves.
Let's invent a name for him, a smile,
a voice which will remain for ever,
a way of planting himself in the world, handsome,
    easy
as if passing aces to fate."
And, of course, we wished him
and he came.
And he turned out to be a handsome, glorious man,
with gel combed hair,
eternal like a God or a record.
The sky began to clear
and his voice sang to us:
    mi Buenos Aires
querido...
It was about six,
a time when the dance halls begin to open
and all the football matches are finished.

Julio Cortázar

A resounding mirror

Until a few days ago, the only argentine memory I could get through my window looking out onto the *rue de Gentilly* was the passage of some sparrow identical to ours, as cheerful, carefree and lazy as those bathing in our fountains or swarming in the dust of our squares.

Now some friends have left me a gramophone and some records of Gardel. You understand at once that you have to listen to Gardel on a gramophone, with all the imaginable distortion and loss; his voice emerges from it as it has been known by the people who were not able to listen to him in person, as it came out from the hallways and living rooms in 1924 or 1925. Gardel-Razzano then: *La cordobesa, El sapo y la comadreja, De mi tierra.* And his voice on its own, loud and full of variations, with the metallic guitars crackling at the bottom of the green and pink loudspeaker: *Mi noche triste, La copa del olvido, El taita del arrabal.* In order to listen to it, the previous ritual seems even necessary, to wind up the gramophone, to adjust the needle. The Gardel of the electric *"pickups"* coincides with his glory, with the movies, with a fame which demanded personal renunciations and treason. It is before, in the patios at *mate* time, during the summer nights, on the old radios that he finds his truth, singing tangos which summarize him and fix him in the memory. Youth prefer the Gardel of *El día que me quieras*, the beautiful voice supported by an orchestra which incites him to put on a pompous voice and to become lyrical. Those of us who have grown up with the friendship of the first records know how much of *Flor de fango* and *Mi Buenos Aires querido, Mi noche triste* and *Sus ojos se cerraron* has been left aside. A change in our moral history is reflected in this change as in many others. The 1920s Gardel contains and expresses the *porteño* who has locked himself in his satisfactory little world: sorrow, treason, misery, are not the weapons yet which will be used as from the next decade by the bitter and frustrated *porteño* and people from the provinces. A last and precarious purity still prevents the melting of the boleros and soap operas. Gardel does not cause, alive, the history which alredy became obvious when he died. He creates affection and admiration, such as

Legui or Justo Suárez; he offers and receives friendship, without any of the shady, erotic reasons supporting the fame of the tropical singers who visit us, or the mere delight in the bad taste and resentful dirt which explain the success of an Alberto Castillo. When Gardel sings a tango, his style expresses that of the people who loved him. The anger or sorrow over the abandonment of a woman are concrete anger and sorrow, related to Juana or Pepa, and not that totally aggressive pretext which is easy to discover in the voice of the hysterical singer of the time, so well adjusted to his audience's hysteria. The different moral tone you can find between *Distant Buenos Aires, you must be so beautiful!* sung by Gardel, and *Adiós, pampa mía!* wailed by Castillo, shows the trend of the change I've just mentioned. The superior arts are not the only ones to reflect a society's process.

I listen to *Mano a mano* one more time, which I prefer to any other tango, and to every recording of Gardel. The lyrics, implacable when assessing the life of a woman who is a prostitute, contain in just a few strophes "the combination of the events" and the infallible prediction of the final decadence. Leaned over this destiny which he shared for a moment, the singer neither expresses anger nor despair. Full of sadness, he evokes her and sees that in her poor borderline life she was just a good woman. Until the end, despite appearances, he will defend the essential honesty of his old friend. And he will wish her the best, stressing his view:

> *I hope the man who will support you will have lasting money,*
> *that you'll back out from reveler pimps,*
> *and that the guys will say: "She's a good woman".*

Perhaps I prefer this tango because it shows exactly what Carlos Gardel really represents. If his songs touched every level of the popular sentimentalism, all the way from the irremissible rancor, to the joy of singing for the sake of singing, from the celebration of turf glories to the account of a police event, the happy medium within which his art falls for ever is that of this almost contemplative tango, of a calmness we have inevitably lost. If this balan-

TEMPORADA
1996

PIERRE MONETTE
LE GUIDE DU
TANGO

Poster of Gotán. *Susana Rinaldi,
november of 1996.*

Cover of Le Guide du Tango *by
Pierre Monette.*

ce was precarious, and demanded the emergence of low sensuality and poor humor oo-
zing out of the loudspeakers and popular records, the truth is that Gardel marked its most
beautiful point, for many of us a final and irre-
coverable moment. An Argentina which is not
easy to recall is reflected in his voice of a *porteño compadre.*

I want to leave this page with two anecdotes
which I think are beautiful and fair. The first is
the intention of —and, I hope, a good lesson
for— the starchy musicologists. In a restaurant
on rue Montmartre, between with one plate of
clams and another, I ended up talking to Jane
Bathori about my great affection for Gardel. I
learned then that they had traveled once in the
same plane. "What did you think of Gardel?", I
asked. Bathori's voice —this voice which had
sung the quintessence of Debussy, Fauré and
Ravel— answered me overwhelmed by emotion: *"Il était charmant, tout à fait charmant.
C'était un plaisir de causer avec lui".* And, later,
in all sincerity: *"Et quelle voix!"*

The other anecdote has been told by Alberto Girri, and I believe it's a perfect summary of the admiration of our people for their
singer. A movie theater in a southern district
shows the film *Cuesta abajo*, and a porteño,
wearing a scarf, was waiting for the moment
to enter the theater. An acquaintance of his
questions him from the street: 'Are you going
to the movies? What are they showing?' And
the other, calmly answers: 'They're showing
one of the "mute"...' (nickname populary
used for Gardel).

Poster of Gotán. *Gardel l' immortel.
Revision of traditional and contemporary
tango in Europe. December, 1993.*

La Revue du Tango Traditionnel et Contemporain

11 décembre

Gardel
l'immortel

Hermenegildo Sábat: a tribute of the Gobierno de la Ciudad de Buenos Aires in the centenary of Gardel's birth.

Bibliography:

Arlt, Roberto: *Los siete locos*; Claridad, Buenos Aires, 1929.

Benarós, León. "El tango y los lugares y casas de baile", en *La historia del tango,* T. II; Corregidor, Buenos Aires, 1977.

Bioy Casares, Adolfo: *El sueño de los héroes*; Emecé, Buenos Aires, 1989.

Blázquez, Eladia: *Cancionero*; Torres Agüero editor, Buenos Aires, 1982.

Borges, Jorge Luis: *Obras completas*; Emecé, Buenos Aires, 1974.

Bose, Walter B. L.; Sáenz, Julio C: *Sellos postales argentinos con historia*; Manrique Zago ediciones, Buenos Aires, 1981.

Bossio, Jorge; Brughetti, Romualdo y otros (textos y comentarios): *Arte bajo la ciudad*; Manrique Zago ediciones, Buenos Aires, 1978.

Cadícamo, Enrique: *Poemas del bajo fondo. Viento que lleva y trae*; Peña Lillo, Buenos Aires, 1964.

Camino, Miguel A: *Chaquiras*; Buenos Aires, 1926.

Carella, Tulio: *El sainete criollo, Antología*; Hachette, Buenos Aires, 1957.

Castillo, Cátulo y otros (textos); Alonso, Carlos y otros (plástica): *Lastima bandoneón*; Ediciones Hualen, Buenos Aires, 1975.

Cortázar, Julio: *La vuelta al día en ochenta mundos*; Siglo XXI, Buenos Aires, 1967.

Costantini, Humberto: *Cuestiones con la vida*; Galerna, Buenos Aires, 1984.

Couselo, Jorge M.: Etchegaray, Natalio P. y otros (textos); Salatino, Jorge (fotografía): *Buenos Aires ciudad tango*; Manrique Zago ediciones. Buenos Aires, 1986.

De la Púa, Carlos: *La crencha engrasada*; Porteña, Buenos Aires, 1954.

Del Mazo, Marcelino: *Los vencidos*, 2da. serie; Buenos Aires, 1910.

Discépolo, Enrique Santos: *Cancionero*; Torres Agüero editor, Buenos Aires, 1977.

Eichelbaum, Samuel: *Un guapo del 900*; Buenos Aires, 1939.

Escardó, Florencio: *Geografía de Buenos Aires*; Eudeba, 1966.

Etchebarne, Miguel D.: *Juan Nadie. Vida y muerte de un compadre*; Alpe, Buenos Aires, 1957.

Ferrer, Horacio: *Cancionero*; Torres Agüero editor, Buenos Aires, 1980.

Flores, Celedonio: *Chapaleando barro*; El Maguntino, Buenos Aires, 1951.

Flores, Celedonio: *Cancionero*; Torres Agüero editor, Buenos Aires, 1977.

Frank, Waldo: *América hispana*; Buenos Aires, 1931.

Fuentes, Carlos: *Cambio de piel*; Seix Barral, Barcelona, 1967.

Gálvez, Manuel: *Historia de arrabal*; Hachette, Buenos Aires, 1956.

Gálvez, Manuel: *Hombres en soledad*; Buenos Aires, 1937.

Girri, Alberto: *Línea de la vida*; Buenos Aires, 1955.

Gobello, José: *Crónica general del tango*; Fraterna, Buenos Aires, 1980.

Gómez Bas, Joaquín: *Barrio gris*; Buenos Aires, 1952.

Güiraldes, Ricardo: *El cencerro de cristal*; Buenos Aires, 1915.

Ibarguren, Carlos: *De nuestra tierra*; Buenos Aires, 1917.

Keyserling, Conde Hermann von: *Meditaciones sudamericanas*; Buenos Aires, 1931.

Lugones, Leopoldo: *El Payador*; Buenos Aires, 1916.

Marechal, Leopoldo: *Megafón o la guerra*; Sudamericana, Buenos Aires, 1970.

Martínez Estrada, Ezequiel: *Radiografía de la Pampa*; Losada, Buenos Aires, 1957.

Orgambide, Pedro: *Gardel y la patria del mito*; Legasa, Buenos Aires, 1985.

Pastor, Sigfredo (xilografías); Benarós, León y otros (textos): *Buenos Aires tango*; Editorial Quetzal, Buenos Aires, 1966.

Peña, José María (textos y selección de imágenes): *Buenos Aires anteayer*; Manrique Zago ediciones, Buenos Aires, 1983.

Peña, José María (textos y selección de imágenes): *Buenos Aires ayer*; Manrique Zago ediciones, Buenos Aires, 1984.

Portogalo, José: *Letra para Juan Tango*; Buenos Aires, 1957.

Quiñones, Fernando: *Crónicas americanas*; Madrid, 1973.

Rossi, Vicente: *Cosas de negros*; Hachette, Buenos Aires, 1958.

Sabato, Ernesto: *Sobre héroes y tumbas*; Fabril, Buenos Aires, 1961.

Sabato, Ernesto: *Tango, discusión y clave*; Losada, Buenos Aires, 1963.

Salas, Horacio: *Homero Manzi. Antología*; Brújula, Buenos Aires, 1968.

Salas, Horacio: *La poesía de Buenos Aires*; Pleamar, Buenos Aires, 1968.

Salas, Horacio: *Conversaciones con Raúl González Tuñón*; La Bastilla, Buenos Aires, 1975.

Salas, Horacio: *El tango*; Planeta, Buenos Aires, 1986.

Salas, Horacio: *El Tango. Una guía definitiva*; Aguilar, Buenos Aires, 1996.

Scalabrini Ortiz, Raúl: *El hombre que está solo y espera*; Albatros, Buenos Aires, 1951.

Soler Cañas, Luis: *Orígenes de la literatura lunfarda*; Siglo XX, Buenos Aires, 1961.

Soler Cañas, Luis; Gobello, José: *Primera antología lunfarda*; Buenos Aires, 1965.

Silva Valdés, Fernán: *Tango*; Buenos Aires, 1930.

Tallon, José Sebastián: *El tango en sus etapas de música prohibida*; Amigos del Libro Argentino, Buenos Aires, 1964.

Vega, Carlos: *Danzas y canciones argentinas. Teorías e investigaciones*; Est. Gráfico Ferrero, Buenos Aires, 1936.

Verbitsky, Bernardo: *Calles de tango*; Buenos Aires, 1953.

Photographs by:

Jorge Luis Campos: Cover and Backcover/Pág. 14/15, 17, 20/21, 57, 61, 79, 99, 131, 132, 134, 135, 137. *Jack Tucmanián:* Pág. 24/25, 35, 41, 65, 85, 99, 102, 105, 111, 112, 128, 132, 142/143, 144/145, 150/151. *Archivo Gráfico de la Nación:* Pág. 8/9, 12/13, 36/37, 43, 47/48, 53, 63, 71, 82/83, 87, 90/91, 96, 97, 117 ab., 118/119/120/121. *Horacio Forlano:* Pág. 39. *Graciela García Romero:* Pág. 92, 130. *Elizabeth Goujon:* Pág. 80/81. *Eduardo Longont:* Pág. 114. *S. Rimathé:* Pág. 26, 51, 53 ab., 66/67, 75/76, 117 arr. *Pedro Roth:* Pág. 85, 126. *Jorge Salatino:* 69, 88, 98, 107, 109, 137.

Summary

Mural painting in Parque Patricios: El tango en la calle.

No matter how, everything here is in
motion and as in labor agitation. Then,
my fellow countrymen, let's start again!
That's what Herodotus, great lantern of
History who knew a lot, recommended.
And good-bye! I'm leaving!

Leopoldo Marechal

TANGO
POETRY OF BUENOS AIRES

se terminó de imprimir en julio de 1998.
Impresión: Mateu Cromo, España.
Fotocromía: M^cNA Digital, Argentina.
Tirada: 3.000 ejemplares